Franz-Günter Winkler

Spacetime Holism

Franz-Günter Winkler

Spacetime Holism

A Fundamental Approach to the Representation Problem in Cognitive Science

Südwestdeutscher Verlag für Hochschulschriften

Impressum/Imprint (nur für Deutschland/ only for Germany)
Bibliografische Information der Deutschen Nationalbibliothek: Die Deutsche Nationalbibliothek verzeichnet diese Publikation in der Deutschen Nationalbibliografie; detaillierte bibliografische Daten sind im Internet über http://dnb.d-nb.de abrufbar.
Alle in diesem Buch genannten Marken und Produktnamen unterliegen warenzeichen-, marken- oder patentrechtlichem Schutz bzw. sind Warenzeichen oder eingetragene Warenzeichen der jeweiligen Inhaber. Die Wiedergabe von Marken, Produktnamen, Gebrauchsnamen, Handelsnamen, Warenbezeichnungen u.s.w. in diesem Werk berechtigt auch ohne besondere Kennzeichnung nicht zu der Annahme, dass solche Namen im Sinne der Warenzeichen- und Markenschutzgesetzgebung als frei zu betrachten wären und daher von jedermann benutzt werden dürften.

Verlag: Südwestdeutscher Verlag für Hochschulschriften Aktiengesellschaft & Co. KG
Dudweiler Landstr. 99, 66123 Saarbrücken, Deutschland
Telefon +49 681 37 20 271-1, Telefax +49 681 37 20 271-0, Email: info@svh-verlag.de
Zugl.: Wien, TU, Diss, 2004

Herstellung in Deutschland:
Schaltungsdienst Lange o.H.G., Berlin
Books on Demand GmbH, Norderstedt
Reha GmbH, Saarbrücken
Amazon Distribution GmbH, Leipzig
ISBN: 978-3-8381-0418-8

Imprint (only for USA, GB)
Bibliographic information published by the Deutsche Nationalbibliothek: The Deutsche Nationalbibliothek lists this publication in the Deutsche Nationalbibliografie; detailed bibliographic data are available in the Internet at http://dnb.d-nb.de.
Any brand names and product names mentioned in this book are subject to trademark, brand or patent protection and are trademarks or registered trademarks of their respective holders. The use of brand names, product names, common names, trade names, product descriptions etc. even without a particular marking in this works is in no way to be construed to mean that such names may be regarded as unrestricted in respect of trademark and brand protection legislation and could thus be used by anyone.

Publisher:
Südwestdeutscher Verlag für Hochschulschriften Aktiengesellschaft & Co. KG
Dudweiler Landstr. 99, 66123 Saarbrücken, Germany
Phone +49 681 37 20 271-1, Fax +49 681 37 20 271-0, Email: info@svh-verlag.de

Copyright © 2009 by the author and Südwestdeutscher Verlag für Hochschulschriften Aktiengesellschaft & Co. KG and licensors
All rights reserved. Saarbrücken 2009

Printed in the U.S.A.
Printed in the U.K. by (see last page)
ISBN: 978-3-8381-0418-8

Contents

Introduction 1
Purpose and Structure of the Thesis 4
1   The Foundations of Spacetime Holism 8
   1.1   Introduction 8
   1.2   David Bohm's Holism 8
   1.3   Inside Versus Outside Views 10
   1.4   The Universe as one Spacetime Whole 13
   1.5   Infinite Complexity and Self-Containment 14
   1.6   Spacetime Structure and the Duality Relation 15
   1.7   Summary 19
2   Self-Organizing Systems 20
   2.1   Introduction 20
   2.2   Self-Organization and Holism 20
   2.3   The *System* From the Viewpoint of Spacetime Holism 21
   2.4   Emergence 24
   2.5   Overlapping Systems – a Road to Holism 25
   2.6   Part-Whole Containment in Dynamical Systems 27
   2.7   Summary 30
3   Spacetime and Relativity Theory 32
   3.1   Introduction 32
   3.2   The Normalization Problem of Special Relativity 32
   3.3   The Interpretation of Special Relativity 50
   3.4   Towards a Euclidean General Relativity 61
   3.5   Summary 69
4   Information Processing 71
   4.1   Introduction 71
   4.2   The Unity of Information and Processing 71
   4.3   The Duality Between Meaning and Computation 73
   4.4   A Hypothesis on the Divergence of AI Research 73
   4.5   Summary 85
5   The Representation Problem 86
   5.1   Two Aspects of Representations 86
   5.2   Representationalism and the Computational Theory of Mind 86
   5.3   The Critics of Representationalism 87
   5.4   Spacetime Holism and the Representation Problem 91
   5.5   Semantics, Meaning and Causal Effect 96
   5.6   The Chinese Room 102
   5.7   Generalizing the Concept of Representation 103
   5.8   Summary 104
6   The Hard Problem of Consciousness 105
   6.1   Introduction 105
   6.2   Easy Versus Hard Problems 105
   6.3   Object, Self and Psychophysical Link 106
   6.4   Solving the Hard Problem 108
   6.5   Representation, Intentionality and Qualia 110
   6.6   Duality Between Inside and Outside Views 111
   6.7   Summary 113

7 The Passage of Time 115
   7.1 Introduction 115
   7.2 What is the Problem of the Passage of Time? 115
   7.3 Spacetime Holism and the Asymmetry of Time 116
   7.4 The Contributions of Spacetime Holism 117
   7.5 Infinite Complexity and Structural Containment 117
   7.6 How Time Passes 118
   7.7 Summary 120
8 Conclusion 121
References 123

Introduction

Spacetime holism is an ambitious project. If there was something like a consistent and well-accepted scientific world view, it would be nothing less than the attempt to develop an alternative. However, there is no such thing. Instead, science is a patchwork of views and theories that hardly fit together. As long as we are interested in solutions to well-defined problems in well-defined domains, science does a great job. In answering the big questions, though, it keeps failing. Some prominent examples addressed in this thesis are connected with the understanding of human cognition, the relation between mind and matter, and the riddles of time.

Spacetime holism does not claim that the dominating scientific paradigms and theories are just wrong, but it points at alternative ways to interpret them. It does make a difference whether we hold that "cognition *is* information processing", or just say that "it is useful to model cognition under the paradigm of information processing". In the first case different approaches to cognition either can be embedded into the information processing paradigm, or – in the final consequence - have to be plain wrong. In the second case, other approaches can be useful as well. Does this open the door for complete arbitrariness? How can it be that incompatible views of the same problem are useful at the same time? Spacetime holism asks and tries to answer these questions.

There is, however, a price to pay for the new perspective. The necessary giving up of deep-rooted habits of thought may be regarded by many as too high a price. Nevertheless, the foundations for the suggested change of mind in science can be found everywhere (from theoretical physics to systems theory and philosophy) – what is so often missing, though, is the drawing of the radical conclusions, e.g. "quantum theory is really strange and interesting, but – thank God – it is irrelevant in our macro-world."

Of course, there are lots of friends and foes for spacetime holism, but mostly this simple scheme does not work. A good example is radical constructivism that so nicely criticizes representationalism (the still ruling paradigm in cognitive science and source of many problems), and that incorporates important holistic features, but fails to take the decisive step towards a truly holistic theory. Another example is relativity theory that comes up with the notion of the so-called spacetime continuum, but falls short of providing an understandable interface for more general theorizing about the connection of space and time.

As has already become clear, this thesis is about many problems in many domains, maybe too many from the traditional understanding of a scientific thesis: "Select a well-defined problem, collect what is state of the art, and show what can be improved." From a holistic perspective, however, things cannot be analyzed separately. The strength of the suggested approach does not primarily come from a rigorous, inescapable string of arguments in one domain, but from the fact that one-and-the-same view opens up perspectives for the solution of problems in many different domains.

The above said does not imply that scientific criteria are not met. The essential arguments have been published in their respective scientific domains. This, of course, meant that compromises had to be made, and that the big picture could not be fully conveyed. This thesis, however, is a chance to show how things fit together.

The following short chapter, which deals with the purpose and structure of the thesis, aims at making clear that the thesis does represent a whole, despite the fact that the single chapters are about seemingly very different topics from different domains.

After introducing the basic concepts of spacetime holism (1 The Foundations of Spacetime Holism) I will show how spacetime holism is inspired by and helps to understand the concepts associated with the theory of self-organization (2 Self-Organizing Systems). A crucial chapter is devoted to relativity theory, or better, an alternative interpretation of relativity theory (3 Spacetime and Relativity). This, indeed, is a very essential part, as one of the seemingly strangest suggestions of spacetime holism, namely the full integration of space and time, requires a basis in theoretical physics. The paradigm of information processing is criticized in chapter 4 (Information Processing), where the inseparability of information and processing as well as a duality relation between computation and meaning are suggested.

The succeeding chapters show spacetime holism's account of problems that seem unsolvable from the traditional scientific perspective. In chapter 5 (The Representation Problem) a far-reaching problem of cognitive science is addressed, namely the question in which way what is inside a cognitive system is related to the outside. Once in the domain of the philosophy of mind, I suggest a solution to its most fundamental problem concerning the place of consciousness in the material world (6 The Hard Problem of Consciousness). This might be regarded as a natural final chapter, but it still is a necessary basis for something else, namely spacetime holism's account of the so-called passage of time (7 The Passage of Time).

At the end of this introduction, I would like to point out how the content of this thesis, i.e. the suggested world view, is reflected in the structure of the thesis. The problem of inseparability and its implications for the open field of investigation has already been mentioned. Another important point is circularity and self-containment, which are on the one hand central features of spacetime holism, and which on the other hand permeate the argumentation. What forms a basic assumption (e.g. the duality between inside and outside concepts of observation) reappears as an outcome (an account of how outside views are constructed from inside views).

Unlike in traditional scientific reasoning, circularity and self-containment are taken as measures of quality. A theory or worldview as far-reaching as spacetime holism must be applicable to itself and thus must be able to say something about itself.

Purpose and Structure of the Thesis

At first glance, this thesis might look like a patchwork of more or less independent chapters dealing with problems in very different domains. In fact, some of the parts tell their own stories and should thus be understandable in the context of the first two foundational chapters alone. From a more abstracted point of view, however, the parts do form an integrated whole. It is the aim of this overview to make clear what this whole is and how it is served by the parts. I will try to make the central points by asking and answering some elementary questions about the thesis.

What is the purpose of the thesis?

The purpose of the thesis is to formulate the worldview of spacetime holism, to show its compatibility with the theory of self-organization and relativity theory, and its potential to answer the hardest of the unsolved questions on the borderline between science and philosophy in a consistent way. The focus of argumentation is formed by the so-called representation problem of cognitive science.

What is the problem to be resolved?

The general problem of the thesis might be called the world view problem: "Do we have a (scientific) world view that provides a perspective to address the big questions centering around human cognition and consciousness in a consistent way?"

The representation problem in cognitive science contains all these questions or is at least strongly connected to them. In short, the representation problem is the question in which way what is inside a natural cognitive system is related to the outside.

What is well-known?

It is well-known that the above mentioned world view problem is unsolved. For the case of cognitive science, it is well known that the different paradigms stressing different aspects of cognition are incompatible. In addition to that, there is no account of meaning which explains how mental states can be meaningful for the system that holds these mental states.

What is the novelty?

Though being based on a known holistic approach (David Bohm's "Undivided Wholeness"), there are enough differences justifying to regard spacetime holism as a new philosophical approach.

The key argument for the solution of the representation problem is borrowed from dynamical systems theory. The general view of cognition, however, which makes this argument applicable, is new.

The suggested interpretation of relativity theory in the spirit of spacetime holism is new, as well as the approach to the so-called "hard problem of consciousness" and the proposed understanding of the passage of time.

What are the results obtained and why are they better than other solutions?
Generally speaking, the result obtained is the worldview of spacetime holism, which is suggested to be better than other worldviews, because it offers solutions where there were no solutions before while saving the benefits of the known and (partially) successful paradigms.

In the domain of cognitive science, the achieved result is an account of the representation problem that dissolves the tensions between the known paradigms and explains how mental representations can be meaningful.

What is the relation between the whole of the thesis and its parts?
When a new worldview is suggested, it is supposed to pass an almost unlimited number of tests from all possible domains and disciplines. This, of course, not only goes beyond the scope of a single thesis – in a strong sense it can never be fulfilled. Does this mean that any attempt to suggest a new scientific worldview is a useless undertaking? Hopefully not!

In this situation, it is the crucial question how a maximum of support for the new worldview can be compiled in the limited format of a scientific writing. As a mixed strategy, this thesis tries to obey the following imperatives, which define the roles of the chapters.

Find a level of argumentation that lies between the disciplines
It is important to stress that the core of spacetime holism does not lie in some specific scientific discipline (like physics or cognitive science). Spacetime holism's key concepts are defined on an abstract level showing some equidistance to the disciplines they are applied to. In chapter 1, spacetime holism is developed on the basis of the holistic philosophy of David Bohm.

Find a center of argumentation
The representation problem of cognitive science perfectly qualifies as a center of argumentation, because it reflects all the aspects of what has been termed the world view problem. In a more rigorous manner than for the other topics of the thesis, it is shown what the state of the art is and how the known fundamental problems can be tackled by spacetime holism.

The suggested approach to the representation problem is made sharp in chapter 5. There are, however, important connections to the following chapters:
- o In chapter 2, the notion of "overlapping systems" and the concept of "embedding" are introduced, which form the basis of spacetime holism's account of representation.

- In chapter 4, the still ruling paradigm in cognitive science, namely information processing, is criticized. In the domain of computer chess it is shown that meaning and computation, which are the central ideas standing behind the assumption of mental representations, are inseparable. By this, the need for an approach different to that of information processing can be concluded.
- In chapter 6, it is shown that the suggested approach to representation, unlike all known approaches, does provide a perspective to address the issue of consciousness.
- In chapter 7, spacetime holism's concept of representation is applied to the time dimension, which allows to formulate an account of the passage of time.

Look for related theories, show the connections and differences
A related theory is David Bohm's holism, which is even used as a starting point in chapter 1. The main difference between Bohm's approach and spacetime holism is given by the treatment of time, which plays an important role for the interpretation of relativity theory (chapter 3) and finally for the suggested approach to the passage of time (chapter 7).

There is, however, a second "theory" with strong connections to spacetime holism, namely the theory of self-organizing systems. By showing how the two fit together (chapter 2) spacetime holism inherits all the domains, in which the theory of self-organizing systems is successfully applied. In the same place it is shown how spacetime holism solves the fundamental problems attached to the theory of self-organization, thereby making clear what the difference is.

Show where the shortcomings of the traditional approaches are and dissolve them
The work standing behind this thesis has been driven by the recognition of shortcomings, both on the level of specific disciplines and on the level of the overall scientific world view. Although it has been attempted to show the problems in a way similar to how they are perceived by the scientific community, the focus has been on reformulating the problems. In fact, the formulation of a problem implicitly contains lots of prejudices that very often prevent solutions right from the start. One of the major benefits of spacetime holism is that it allows surprising reformulations of known problems (in terms of space and time structures), thus making synoptic views and rather simple (dis)solutions possible. Only by being reformulated, the many problems from so different disciplines become accessible in a single thesis.

Go for the critical questions
For spacetime holism it is not only important to make the differences to known paradigms explicit, but also to address the most critical implications of its new assumptions. The inseparability of space and time could be argued for on e.g. a systems theoretical level alone. However, there would not be

much gain for an overall scientific world view, if the postulated integration of space and time could not be made compatible with relativity theory (chapter 3). Other critical questions dealt with in this thesis concern the issue of consciousness (chapter 6) and the issue of the passage of time (chapter 7). While it is a major drawback of traditional scientific approaches to have blind spots when it comes to these two questions, spacetime holism offers rather simple solutions.

Although the basic assumptions of spacetime holism were formulated with an eye on quantum theory, it has to be admitted that the critical question how spacetime holism and quantum theory go together is not fully answered in this thesis.

1 The Foundations of Spacetime Holism

Contribution to the Thesis
On the basis of David Bohm's holism, the foundations of spacetime holism are laid. The minimal conceptual framework is defined on an abstract level. The distinction between inside and outside views is used for a discussion of the scientific method.

1.1 Introduction

Spacetime holism is the outcome of a long personal process of inquiry into the problems which form the main chapters of this thesis. Beside the confrontation with systems theory (especially dynamical systems and self-organizing systems) and the philosophy of radical constructivism,[1] a key input to this process was David Bohm's book "Wholeness and the Implicate Order."[2]. Though I will use different concepts and a terminology more apt for addressing the problems I am concerned with, and though there are also significant differences in the treatment of e.g. time and spacetime integration, I would like to point both at the importance of Bohm's influence on my work, and at the basic compatibility between his approach and mine.

It is therefore natural to start this chapter with an overview of Bohm's holism, before laying the foundations of spacetime holism.

1.2 David Bohm's Holism

David Bohm is mostly known for his controversial interpretation of quantum theory.[3] However, his work as a philosopher is probably much more important.

His starting point is the understanding of the universe as an unbroken, undivided whole. Every attempt to analyze the whole by breaking it into seemingly independent parts is in principle incomplete and in the last consequence doomed to failure. Of course, it does make sense for limited purposes to treat the "the various patterns that can be abstracted" from the whole - as they show a "relative autonomy and stability" - as separately existing things. However, that should not lead us to believe in the fragmented nature of the universe, which is so obviously held not only in science, but which permeates our whole existence as human beings.

Bohm very strongly points out that everything or, better, the whole is in constant motion, is evolving, and that nothing ever is fixed or reaches an ultimate, final form. Some of the notions and phrases underlining the processuality in his thinking are "undivided wholeness in flowing

---
[1] See (Förster, 1985; Glasersfeld, 1990; Maturana & Varela, 1987; Schmidt, 1987; Schmidt, 1992).
[2] (Bohm, 1980)
[3] His interpretation is based on the assumption of non-local hidden variables (Bohm, 1951; Bohm & Hiley 1993).

movement" or "holomovement", "the enfolding-unfolding universe"; he also stresses that "knowledge should be considered as a process".

When Bohm introduces his central concepts of *order*, *measure* and *structure*, the processual character is underlined, indicating that it is always an act of orde*ring*, measu*ring* and structu*ring* performed by somebody, and that things are not just out there in a fixed and objectifyable form.

The concept of *order* is developed on the basis of the notions *similarity* and *difference*. Order is thus a similarity of differences, or the other way around, a difference between similarities. Higher degrees of order are to be understood as meta-similarities respectively meta-differences. As an example for an order of the first degree he considers a line holding points A, B, C etc. in constant distances. The order of the line is the similarity between the differences of the positions of these points. The difference between the points A and B is similar to the difference between the points B and C. A higher degree of order is necessary to characterize curves, where there is a difference between the differences between A and B, and B and C. However, there may be meta-similarities between such meta-differences, e.g. the difference between A-B and B-C can be similar to the difference between B-C and C-D.

This game can be played ad infinitum leading to orders of infinite degree.[4] The universe holds such an order of infinite degree.

The concept of *measure* is understood much in the sense of the root of the word meaning *limit*. Thus, to measure means to put into limits. *Structure* is measured order, i.e. order put into limits. A wall is the measured order of the bricks, a room is the measured order of walls, a house is the measured order of rooms, etc.[5]

When it comes to formulating the relation between the infinite structure and the whole of space and time, Bohm is both clear and radical:

"Indeed, in principle, this structure extends over the whole universe and over the whole past, with implications for the whole future,"[6] and shortly after that: "This order is not to be understood solely in terms of a regular arrangement of *objects* (e.g. in rows) or as a regular arrangement of *events* (e.g. in a series). Rather, a *total order* is contained, in some implicit sense, in each region of space and time."[7]

By *implicit* (or *implicate*) order he means enfolded order, by explicit (or explicate) order he means unfolded order. The flowing movement of the whole can thus be understood as a process of

---

[4] For Bohm, there is no randomness, but just order of infinite degree.
[5] (Bohm, 1980), p. 120
[6] (Bohm, 1980), p. 148
[7] (Bohm, 1980), p. 149

continuous enfolding and unfolding of order or structure. A good example for *implication* and *explication* are plants and their seeds; another one is human memory: The storage of experiences in the human brain is a process of enfolding, while the recalling of memories is a process of unfolding.

The relations of spacetime holism to Bohm's "Undivided Wholeness" will become evident in the course of this chapter. However, there are also significant differences that justify the use of a different terminology. Although I agree with the importance of considering processes rather than static entities, I am aiming at a more radical view of time that underlines the full integration with space. Unlike it seems to be the case in Bohm's philosophy, I do not take the flow of time as given, but I try to derive it from structural properties of the spacetime whole, which cannot be formulated in Bohm's terminology. Another important reason for the change of terminology is the possibility to formulate an interface to systems theory, especially to the theory of self-organization, and consequently to make the theory and its statements comparable to known approaches in cognitive science and the philosophy of mind.

1.3 Inside Versus Outside Views

To put the distinction between inside and outside views at the beginning of my introduction to spacetime holism is far from being an arbitrary choice. Like a thread, the topic connects all parts of the thesis, be it relativity theory, the representation problem, consciousness, or time.

Although the application of the inside-outside distinction sheds new light on many different scientific and philosophical approaches, it is a very trivial distinction.

By *outside view* I mean the ideal of natural science, namely the construction of a God-like perspective of the world, where observation is no longer a physical, interactive process. From the outside, we see things "as they are". However, all our observations are inside operations, as we are part of the physical universe, and each observation, in the last consequence, comes down to an interaction between observer and thing observed.

As a first example, think of a simple length measurement of an object by the use of a meter stick. The statement "this object is one meter long" says something about the object, the meter stick and the measurement procedure, and is therefore the result of an inside observation (using a "meter" stick that is twice as long would yield half a meter as a result of the length measurement). Of course, by normalizing measuring instruments and by defining measurement procedures we may construct a perfectly useful outside perspective, which allows us to treat the result of a measurement as an objective property of the measured object. This is much less clear in the second example: It is hard to think of a statement like "this person is nice" as an outside observer's statement capturing an objective property of a person.

1.3.1 Science and the Construction of Outside Views

Science, especially natural science, can be understood as a huge undertaking to construct an outside view of the universe. Let us take a closer look at science's methods which clearly show how the construction of an outside view is achieved in science.

Isolation of the Investigated Phenomenon From its Surroundings

Maybe the first step for scientific investigation is the definition of the object of investigation. This separation of an object and its context is already a highly problematic cut for a holistic approach. In some sense, the object is created by this cut. The fact that scientific experiments are performed ideally in a laboratory reflects this essential separation.

Definition of the Interaction Between Observer and Thing Observed

Only a well-defined set of interactions is allowed to take place between the observer (respectively the observation tools) and the thing observed. These interactions are called measurement procedures.

Normalization of Measuring Instruments

A precondition for any useful measurement is the normalization of measuring instruments. Otherwise it does not make any sense to relate the results of different experiments to each other. The meter stick used in an experiment in Japan must be in a well-defined sense the same as the meter stick used in an experiment in France; a meter stick should still have the same length when e.g. the temperature changes.

Quantification Over Space and Time

The less it is possible to isolate the investigated object from its environment or context, and the less it is possible to define the measurement procedure, the higher is the importance of repeating experiments in different places and contexts by different observers (e.g. different scientific staff and different laboratories). In the so-called soft sciences, where even the object of investigation is very hard to define, where contexts cannot be fully cut away, and even the measurement tools and procedures are not well-definable (think, e.g. of the problem of translating a questionnaire), the importance of quantification becomes dominant (i.e. the statisticians take over).

This illustration of the scientific method is not meant as a critique – I know of no better way to construct outside views. However, there is a high degree of unawareness of the fact that scientific observation inescapably is still an inside operation. To equate the constructed outside perspective with something like *reality-as-it-is*, is nothing but ideological belief from the viewpoint of spacetime holism, and the main source of deep philosophical problems, not only in cognitive science. One of the aims of this thesis is to show that such naïve realism simply does not work.

An often criticized method in the social sciences is worth mentioning in the context of inside observation. In feminist philosophy of science[8] there seems to be very clear understanding of the problems connected with the scientific methods of constructing outside views. A good example is the suggested *qualitative* method of interviewing. Rather than trying to avoid what cannot be avoided, namely the involvement of the observer in the measurement, the interviewer very consciously creates an interactive situation that she or he does not fully control. If these investigations are performed by well-trained interviewers, and if the analysis of the protocols is done in a highly careful way, such qualitative methods may produce much better results (at least in certain domains) than quantitative methods, which cannot even investigate many phenomena due to the impossibility to define them.

1.3.2 Systems Theoretical Formulation

In order to make spacetime holism applicable in a wide range of domains, the connection of the used concepts to systems theory is of central importance. As a first step, I suggest to understand the result of an inside observation as the product of a *system* consisting of the observer (respectively the measurement tools), the thing observed and the measurement procedures. In this place, I will not specifying the term system, nor will I talk about systems theoretical properties relevant for the elaboration of an account of inside observation. However, I would like to indicate that this move to systems theory – as simple as it may seem – together with the drawing of the radical consequences, already paves the way for the alternative solutions to the problems in cognitive science and the philosophy of mind, which will be suggested throughout this thesis.

1.3.3 Relations to Theoretical Physics

To a certain extent, there is some awareness for the problems connected with the distinction between inside and outside concepts of observation in theoretical physics. In quantum theory, respectively in its interpretations,[9] the so-called Heisenberg cut[10] is described as the cut between the investigated object and the measurement apparatus. The problems of another cut, namely that between an object and its surroundings, is already implied by the notion of quantum entanglement.

There is also felt a growing need for making a distinction between different types of views or models. However, the pairs *inside-outside* or *endo-exo* are used in very different ways and with very different ideas standing behind them.[11]

---

[8] (Stanley & Wise, 1983)
[9] For an overview, see (Jammers, 1974).
[10] For a discussion, see (Primas, 1993).
[11] See (Atmanspacher & Daalenort, 1994); the contribution of Svozil (1994) matches best with the suggested use of the inside-outside distinction.

In physics, the inside-outside distinction almost exclusively appears in the context of quantum mechanics. In a limited way, interpretations of relativity theory in the spirit of Lorentz show some awareness for the two types of observation, while the standard interpretation seems to be ignorant. In chapter 3 I will elaborate an alternative interpretation of relativity theory on the basis of a clear treatment of the inside-outside distinction.

1.3.4 Does Spacetime Holism Provide an Outside View?

The answer to this question is basically *yes*. While stressing the impossibility of actually taking the position of an outside observer of the universe, and while pointing at the problems arising from that, spacetime holism can be understood as an attempt to construct an outside view of the universe, at least conceptually. As a critical analysis of the basic structural notions (like continuity and discontinuity) introduced in the following shows, one question can never be fully answered: Do these notions capture objective properties of the spacetime whole?

Rather than trying to sneak around this problem, I will use this opportunity to formulate spacetime holism's attitude towards itself. Spacetime holism is fully aware of being a construction. Therefore its concepts cannot be taken as objective or final. Spacetime holism does not start from saying that the universe *is* a spacetime whole, what is meant, instead, is that it is assumed (and shown) that it does make sense to look at the universe *as* a spacetime whole. The claim, though, is very strong, namely that spacetime holism is a better outside view in the sense that it allows a more complete and more consistent description of the universe, not having to halt in front of some intriguing philosophical problems as traditional approaches so obviously have to.

For spacetime holism, the two-way relation between inside and outside views is very important. On the one hand, any outside view must be understood as a construction on the basis of inside observations, on the other hand, inside observation (and the act of constructing an outside perspective) is looked at from an outside observer's perspective. This circularity is inescapable for spacetime holism, but not vicious. Quite to the contrary, this circle, if it can be shown to be self-supporting, should be regarded as sign of quality, for it shows the capacity of the theory to say something about itself, which is to be expected from any "theory of theory-making".

1.4 The Universe as one Spacetime Whole

A difference to Bohm's holism, or at least a point that is not being accounted for by Bohm, is spacetime holism's full integration of space and time.

The idea that space and time form some kind of unity is known to be part of the (standard) interpretation of the theory of relativity. However, there is no common treatment of space and time in other disciplines. The reason for this lies mostly in the big difference between our every-day perceptions of space and of time (time "flows,"[12] space does not), but may also have something to do with the way relativity theory is understood.[13] Though agreeing with known holistic approaches in their treatment of entities and relations in space, I would like to criticize holism for its treatment of the time dimension.

Most holistic approaches are far away from integrating space and time.[14] Instead, time is seen as something special,[15] and different concepts are used for the description of relations in time (e.g. Bohm's "flowing movement", non-determinism in quantum theory, unpredictable emergence in the theory of self-organization). Spacetime holism goes one step further by fully integrating the time dimension: Everything in spacetime must be regarded as one indivisible whole. As a consequence, the same conceptual tools can be applied to both space and time.

1.5 Infinite Complexity and Self-Containment

In accordance with Bohm, I assume the fundamental incompleteness of any description of the whole in terms of perfectly definable parts. This is tantamount to assuming that the (spacetime) whole is infinitely complex (or has an order of infinite degree). From this it follows that an additional feature of the whole can be postulated without running into contradiction, namely the full structural containment of the whole in each location of spacetime. This, again, is already a feature of Bohm's holism as has been pointed out in section 1.2. It does not imply that the structure of the whole can be studied equally well in each part.

Self-containment is a very powerful assumption of which I will make extensive use, especially in chapter 4, where I will introduce spacetime holism's account of the representation problem. There is, however, a high need to demystify the assumption of self-containment, which will be attempted particularly in the context of self-organizing systems in chapter 2. In this place, let me just point to fractal structures,[16] chaos theory,[17] and quantum holography,[18] where self-containment has well-defined meanings.

---

[12] In chapter 7 I will discuss the problem of the passage of time: In the framework of spacetime holism time's flow can be explained as an inside observer's phenomenon – for a hypothetical outside observer of the spacetime whole time is as static as space.
[13] A more intuitive interpretation of relativity theory is suggested in chapter 3.
[14] Though usually not seen as a "holistic" theory, general relativity can be regarded as a prominent exception.
[15] The popularity of „holistic" theories, e.g. theories centering around the notion of self-organization, seems to have a lot to do with their treatment of time. The threat of a completely deterministic or - even worse – a static universe imposed by the traditional scientific world view respectively by relativity theory is countered by a perspective that gives room for chance, creativity, free will and dynamical flow.
[16] See (Mandelbrot, 1987)
[17] For an introduction, see e.g. (Gleick, 1988).
[18] See (Pribram, 1976).

1.6 Spacetime Structure and the Duality Relation

The assumption of infinite complexity of the spacetime whole does not mean that no understanding or description of the structure of spacetime is possible. For my investigation, I suggest a terminology that, on the one hand, allows relations to concepts in mathematics, physics, and systems theory.[19] On the other hand, the terminology is soft enough to be applicable to a wide range of less precise domains, e.g. to psychology and sociology.

1.6.1 Continuity and Discontinuity

I talk about *continuity* along one dimension of a description when the following holds in a rough sense for entities A, B and C:

The relation between A and B is the same as between B and C. Thus, knowing A and its relation to be B means to know about C and possibly a longer sequence of entities.[20]

While *continuity* forms the basis for the recognition of *relations* between entities, *discontinuity* may lead us to make distinctions and to draw borders, it is thus a precondition for the concept of an *object*.

Let us apply this to the physics of space and time. Space and time in special relativity are merely continuous - the existence of the object is taken for granted and is independent of the geometry of space and time. In general relativity discontinuity enters the game - movements are accelerated and objects are introduced as contractions (i.e. discontinuities) of "the spacetime geometry itself."

1.6.2 Structure and Complexity

Continuity and discontinuity come together again when we talk about *structure*. For simple systems we could define structure as a measure for the number of objects and relations (e.g. nodes and links in a semantic network[21]). More interesting systems do not allow a clear separation of objects and relations (e.g. chaotic dynamics), yet we still can measure structure (e.g. in terms of fractal dimensions). A qualitative concept of structure becomes meaningless when there is no continuity (e.g. folk use of the term chaos) as well as when there is no discontinuity (complete order). Structure should thus be understood rather as a product of continuous and discontinuous elements than as a sum. In this sense, there is a strong link to the discussion of the term *complexity*.[22]

---

[19] Especially, I think it is fruitful to link the terminology to different concepts of complexity, see. (Atmanspacher et al. 1992).
[20] The notions continuity and discontinuity can easily be related to Bohm' notions similarity and difference.
[21] See section 4.4, where semantic networks are used as an possible basis for understanding a duality for models of artificial intelligence.
[22] See (Grassberger, 1989).

1.6.3 Levels of Description

The necessity for a distinction between levels of description can be illustrated using the distinction between continuity and discontinuity. What appears as discontinuity on a lower level of description may be described as a continuous sequence of discontinuities on a more abstracted level. An object can be seen as a discontinuity in space - yet there can be a continuous arrangement of objects in space. An event can be seen as a discontinuity in time - yet there can be a continuous sequence of events.

Of course, there is no right level of description. Like the drawing of borders the level of description always depends on the observer's choice.

1.6.4 Non-locality and Locality

The distinction between non-locality and locality is an abstraction of the distinction between continuity and discontinuity. The ideal object has a location in space and is unaffected by its environment. Beside its spatial discontinuity the object is extended in time. Its existence in time is thus not bound to a short interval like it is the case for its spatial existence. In this sense I call objects non-local in time. When reversing space and time we can introduce phenomena that are non-local in space, but local in time. The ideal wave[23] is identical for all (spatial) points. On the time axis there is discontinuity: The behavior of a (spatial) point in a wave is not primarily correlated with prior or later states of that point, but much more to other spatial points (at the same time). Like the objects marks a point in space, the wave marks a point in time.

Some remarks are necessary to put the usage of the terms locality and non-locality into perspective. In quantum theory, non-locality means the relation of entanglement connecting spatially separated parts sharing the same wave function.[24] This connection is made responsible for the instantaneous determinacy of certain aspects also of the distant part when the local part is determined by measurement. Although there are some speculations about "non-locality in time,"[25] the usual understanding of non-locality is restricted to space. In the framework of spacetime holism the notions of locality and non-locality are freed from the narrow context of quantum theory. Though being still applicable to measurement and determination of quantum states, the concepts can now be used for relations in space *and* time, and in very general contexts that are seemingly far away from quantum theory, especially in the context of the theory of self-organization.

---

[23] The metaphorical use of the term "wave" requires some clarification. What I have in mind is a standing wave rather than a propagating one. Associations with quantum theory are intended – the so-called collapse of the wave function shows the postulated properties of spatial non-locality (a simultaneous link between distant parts) and temporal locality (non-predictability, at least from local parameters).
[24] So-called EPR-phenomena (Einstein, Podolsky & Rosen, 1935).
[25] See (Mahler, 1997).

1.6.5 Duality of Spacetime Structure

There will be a lot talk of dualities in the course of this thesis. Indeed, the notion of duality is central to spacetime holism and requires some general remarks. I chose the term *duality* over *dualism*, because I think that dualism has a flavor of contradiction or at least of some impossibility of resolution. When I talk of duality, I always mean the relation between two modes of description that are based on intrinsic faults, i.e. different ways of cutting the spacetime whole. Dualities are resolvable, namely by understanding the infinitely complex nature of the spacetime whole. Duality was chosen over *complementarity*, as complementarity is a highly laden notion that spread from quantum theory[26] to very different domains, including, e.g. complementary medicine, and might provoke unintended associations.

After these remarks, I can formulate the first fundamental duality relation characteristic of spacetime holism:

The First Fundamental Duality Relation

Continuity (non-locality) along one dimension is correlated with discontinuity (locality) along the other dimension.

Only when discontinuity concentrates on the spatial axes, a description as an object is justified. In the same way it is the discontinuity along the time axis that characterizes the wave. Both sides of the duality are necessarily incomplete – in general, there is continuity and discontinuity on all levels in space and time. In the following, I will talk about a duality between particle and wave aspects that correspond with the pairs (*discontinuity in space, continuity in time*) and (*continuity in space, discontinuity in time*).

The classical scientific world view exemplified by Laplace's demon appears as the belief in the sufficiency of the particle aspect:

> *We ought to regard the present state of the universe as the effect of its antecedent state and as the cause of the state that is to follow. An intelligence knowing all the forces acting in nature at a given instant, as well as the momentary positions of all things in the universe, would be able to comprehend in one single formula the motions of the largest bodies as well as the lightest atoms in the world, provided that its intellect were sufficiently powerful to subject all data to analysis; to it nothing would be uncertain, the future as well as the past would be present to its eyes. The perfection that the human mind has been able to give to astronomy affords but a feeble outline of such an intelligence.* (Laplace, 1820)

---

[26] The notion of complementarity was introduced by Niels Bohr (Bohr, 1928).

From this viewpoint time is a purely continuous dimension - there should be a "right" level of description that makes the passage of time a transformation that neither brings anything new nor looses anything.

Of course, quantum theory destroys this picture, but it would be a mistake to assume the viability of the traditional worldview for all other domains or levels of description. Its failure, indeed, is omnipresent.

In science, there is a very general duality between hard and soft sciences: Hard science has to define its concepts (in some description space). It is aiming at forcing arguments and precise predictions - soft science is always context-sensitive (that means, concepts are more associative and thus cannot be localized). Soft science brings together things that seem to be *"very far away"* from each other. Consequently, soft science is less successful in making predictions.

1.6.6 Duality between Levels of Description

In addition to the duality relation between space and time dimensions, I assume a second fundamental duality relation that connects levels of description (respectively scales) in just one dimension:

The Second Fundamental Duality Relation
Continuity (discontinuity) on the lower level of description along one dimension is correlated with discontinuity (continuity) on the higher level of description along the same dimension.

As an intuitive example for this inter-level duality, think of an airplane pilot. The (higher level) freedom of flying through the skies has to be paid with a (lower level) loss of freedom by being tightly fixed and locked in the narrow cockpit. Another example which is connected to time rather than space is the achievement of personal large-scale goals, which usually presupposes the sacrifice of small-scale desires.

Apart from these intuitive examples, the inter-level duality will play an important role in spacetime holism's account of systems properties (see chapter 2).

1.6.7 Causality and Signal

Causality, as might already be clear, plays a secondary role in spacetime holism. Like any other spacetime structures, causes and effects can never be fully identified. However, I would like to use this opportunity to take a closer look at the notion of a *signal* from the perspective of spacetime holism, which is the carrier of causal interactions in a traditional framework.

Both in the form of a moving object or a spreading wave, the signal combines on the one hand spatial and temporal continuity, and on the other hand spatial and temporal discontinuity. While the ideal wave connects points in space simultaneously, and while the resting object connects just points in time, the signal connects points along a spacetime line. As a consequence, discontinuity appears both in space and time dimensions.[27]

Another point that should be raised in the context of causality is its relation to time. Causes and effects differ in chronological order; therefore causality has something to do with the respective understanding of time. Spacetime holism's approach to the asymmetry of time and to the so-called passage of time follows in section 7.

1.6.8 Conservation of Spacetime Structure

As a fundamental background assumption, I supposed - quite in line with Bohm - the full containment of the structure of the whole in each part. The two duality relations just introduced say something about *observed* structure. While in principle it does not make a difference whether the structural properties of continuity and discontinuity appear along space or time dimensions, or on a smaller or larger scale, it is very well important for our models and descriptions.

Quite generally, however, when re-introducing the infinite and omnipresent structure of the whole as the set of structures visible from an infinity of different views, it is only consequent to assume the constancy of this structure everywhere in the spacetime whole. For practical purposes, it is interesting to study how in different situations structure (respectively continuity and discontinuity) is being transformed from space to time or vice versa, or between levels. The latter transformation, of course, is related to Bohm's notions *implication* and *explication*.

1.7 Summary

In this chapter, all of spacetime holism's concepts and assumptions have been introduced. Some of them are borrowed from David Bohm (infinite complexity, inseparability, self-containment), while others are new (distinction between inside and outside views, stress of the inseparability of space and time, duality relations for space and time structures). The distinction between inside and outside views has been used to reformulate important issues in the philosophy of science.

---

[27] In chapter 3 it will be shown how space and time relations change in relativity theory when an object is put into motion.

2 Self-Organizing Systems

Contribution to the Thesis

It is shown how the theory of self-organization can be founded in spacetime holism and how the problems connected with the notions of causality and emergence are thereby dissolved. The concept of embedding is introduced, which will play an important role for spacetime holism's account of the representation problem in cognitive science.

2.1 Introduction

Rather than a fully developed and consistent theory, the theory of self-organization must be understood as a collection of approaches reaching from dynamical systems theory including chaos theory[28] over Hermann Haken's synergetics[29] to radical (biological) constructivism.[30] All of these approaches have in common that they claim to be applicable to a wide variety of scientific disciplines ranging in some cases from physics and chemistry to biology, cognitive science and philosophy. It cannot be the purpose of this chapter to give an introduction or even an overview of the theory of self-organization. Instead, I will look at some of the central concepts in order to show that the theory of self-organization has at least a holistic flavor. However, the decisive step towards a truly holistic theory is not made, which will be regarded as the source of some fundamental problems (e.g. a logically clear treatment of the notion of emergence, and the restriction to hierarchical relations between system levels).

The discussion of these problems is directed at two conclusions. On the one hand the theory of self-organization can be founded in spacetime holism, which automatically solves its hardest problems, and on the other hand the acceptance and consequent application of the central features of self-organizing systems is a king's road to a holistic world view.

2.2 Self-Organization and Holism

The theory of self-organization is usually introduced in the form of a critique of the still ruling reductionist world view. In the following, I will take a closer look at the holistic aspects addressed by the theory of self-organization.

The whole is more than the sum of its parts. This well-known statement reflects that the theory of self-organization is about collective phenomena of systems (which thereby constitute as wholes) that cannot be reduced to the behavior of their parts, at least not in the traditional straightforward way.

---

[28] See (Gleick, 1988).
[29] See (Haken, 1981).
[30] See (Maturana & Varela, 1987).

As a consequence, different forms of part-whole relationships appear. An easy-to-accept concept is *distributed information*, e.g. in neural networks. All parts of the system contribute to all collective information states, such that the parts cannot be given a specific role for the whole. A nice consequence of distributed information is the fact that the loss of a part does not necessarily affect the performance of the whole system.[31]

A key concept for self-organizing systems is *emergence*, which I will critically analyze in section 2.4. The collective behavior of the whole is said to emerge from the interaction of its parts. Depending on the respective interpretation of emergence, there is sometimes also an influence from the emergent level on the level of the parts assumed.

Following from this, there is a lot of confusion about the notion of causality. There is talk about circular causality, efficient versus final cause, bottom up versus top-down causation, weak and strong causality, and non-causality (chance). The critique of the traditional understanding of causality which stands behind these discussions may have well contributed to the popularization of the theory of self-organization, as is addresses the uncomfortable feelings we have with a completely deterministic universe leaving no room for chance and free will. However, scientifically speaking, the messiness of the treatment of causality is a major weakness of the theory of self-organization.

From the perspective of spacetime holism, the theory of self-organization lacks an important aspect of part-whole relationship, namely the full containment of the structure of the whole in each part.

Another important point of critique from a holistic perspective is what could be called the re-introduction of a typical reductionist aspect, namely the restriction to systems hierarchies. Even those approaches, which quite frankly assume top-down causation in addition to bottom-up causation, draw strict hierarchical pictures of system relations (e.g. physical – biological – cognitive – social).[32] This issue will be analyzed in section 2.5.

2.3 The *System* From the Viewpoint of Spacetime Holism

The notion of a system is both central and hard to define, not only in the theory of self-organization. From the perspective of spacetime holism, all that can be done is to describe certain aspects (and their relations), which are relevant for treating something as a system.

(1) External particle aspect. A system shows some independence from its environment and some stability.

---

[31] This property is called "graceful decay."
[32] E.g. (Fuchs, 2003).

(2) External wave aspect. A system is open to the environment; it interacts and thus takes part in multiple meta-systems (hierarchical or overlapping[33]). By this, it is possibly subject to changes.

(3) Internal particle aspect. A system has some internal structure, which can be described as constituent parts in interaction.

(4) Internal wave aspect. A system maintains relations between its parts. ("The whole is more than the sum of its parts").

(5) Representational aspect. The part represents the system; the system represents the meta-system. This aspect has to do with the postulated feature of part-whole containment, it will be discussed in section 2.6 and, in a cognitive context, in chapter 4.

These aspects compete with each other and cannot be fully present at the same time. The more some aspect dominates, the less I am inclined to talk of a self-organizing system. E.g. mere causal systems that can be reduced to the deterministic behavior of their well-definable parts (particle aspect) cannot represent, which presupposes a strong wave aspect.

The aspects (1) to (4), which are linked by the two duality relations described in chapter 1, are illustrated in Fig. 2.1. The illustration is based on the geometrical metaphor of a dominating axis of continuity that may have different spacetime orientations. In the orthogonal direction discontinuity dominates (this reflects the first fundamental duality relation linking continuity and discontinuity in space and time). For the ideal wave the *axis of continuity* is spatial, for the object the *axis of continuity* is temporal. For the wave there are relations in space, for the object there are relations in time. (For a signal, or generally, a moving object, the axis of continuity lies between space and time axes.)

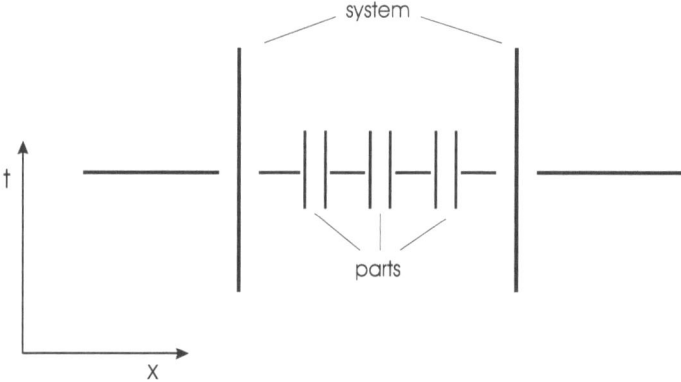

Fig. 2.1. The axes of continuity for the particle and wave aspects of a system.

---

[33] cf. section 2.5.

For different levels of abstraction, continuity and discontinuity along one dimension are related according to the second fundamental duality (the duality between levels). The external particle aspect meaning spatial discontinuity is linked to the internal wave aspect meaning spatial continuity.

Let me use the tools introduced so far to describe certain phenomena in the context of self-organizing systems.

When talking about phase transitions of self-organizing systems, we can distinguish unordered and ordered phases. In an *unordered (chaotic) phase* the dynamical structure is non-local - every point in space shows the same (infinite) structure. The *sensitivity to small influences* can be read as a strong relation between all points in space. Along the time axis there is only a very weak link between subsequent states of a point - we could talk of a lack of (local) determinism. The wave aspect dominates, and the main axis of continuity is spatial.

In an *ordered phase* we observe more or less autonomous structures. Relations between structures in space become less important and relations in time are dominant (local determinism, i.e. the temporal evolution of a spatial entity depends on the entity alone). The particle aspect dominates, and the main axis of continuity is temporal.

As has already been addressed, there is not just one axis of continuity that fully characterizes the state of a process. On different levels of abstraction the axis of continuity may have different orientations. The usual way of dealing with the two contradicting aspects can be described as a strict separation of levels of description. E.g. on the level of energy and matter exchange an *autopoietic system*[34] is *open* to its environment, on the level of its operation or organization the autopoietic system is regarded to be *closed*. For the *radical constructivist*, the consequence of this closed organization is that we are cognitive islands having no access to what is going on outside. Our mental lives are regarded as mere self-products of cognitive systems. Interactions between a cognitive system and its environment (so-called *perturbations*) play only a role as provocations for the system to switch to a different, yet self-determined state. In spactime holism's terminology, this view can be characterized as a stress of the external particle aspect of cognitive organization. The relation between the system and its environment is not addressed in a qualitative manner, there is an informational gap between system and environment, i.e. spatial discontinuity . Along the time axis there is continuity, the main goal of the system being its own survival, i.e. the maintenance of its internal organization (internal wave aspect). The lack of the external wave aspect becomes visible when we talk of social systems.

---

[34] (Maturana&Varela, 1987)

In social sciences there is strong interest in constructivist approaches,[35] but the perception of the benefits of autopoiesis is paralleled by an increasing awareness of its drawbacks. The problem culminates in the question what should be taken as the (autopoietic) system. When starting from the assumption that the cognitive system, i.e. the individual, should be regarded as the primary entity, we loose grasp of the characteristics of the social entity. For spacetime holism, it is highly unclear how a cognitive system that is separated from its environment by an organizational closure should act as an integrative part of a social entity that is supposed to maintain an organization of its own. For a useful concept of a social entity it seems inescapable to postulate a much stronger relation between individuals than just *recursive perturbations*. The individual must *represent* the system whose part it is in order to justify the term *social*.

The alternative assumption, namely the treatment of social processes as autopoietic systems (e.g. Luhmann´s communication systems[36]), faces the problem that the individual can no longer be regarded as a constitutive entity of the system - the individual is placed in the environment and thus plays a subordinate role.

From the viewpoint of spacetime holism there is no real problem, because there cannot be a right description. Both approaches, though incompatible with each other, can be accepted as useful, if only we see their principled incompleteness. The assumption of an operational closure on some level of abstraction is just a distinction that is a necessary condition for the formulation of a model, but makes structure on different levels of abstraction disappear. More on this *problem of overlapping systems* will follow in section 2.5.

2.4 Emergence

Maybe the most mysterious notion in the theory of self-organization is *emergence*. I would like to make a distinction between a weak and a strong meaning of emergence.

The weak meaning, which is compatible with the reductionist picture, simply addresses the observation that a set of functionally describable parts - by interacting with each other - may produce some coherent collective behavior, at least in the eyes of an external observer. The existence of this kind of emergent behavior does no harm to the functional behavior of the parts.

In its strong meaning, the status of emergent phenomena is different - they are supposed to exert effects on the behavior of the parts that produce the behavior. For some scientific hardliners this second interpretation is pure mysticism (see, e.g. Searle's view of emergence),[37] while for the social scientist there seems to be no problem to talk of a bi-directional influence between the level of the

---

[35] (Schmidt, 1992).
[36] (Luhmann, 1987)
[37] (Searle, 1992)

parts and the emergent level of collective behavior. A natural example for this inter-level relation is the relation between individual and society. Society is understood as emerging from interacting individuals and individuals are understood as formed by society. But there can also be given an example from the harder side of science. In Hermann Haken's so-called *synergetics*[38] emergent *order principles* enslave the parts of a system.

What seems to be an irresolvable tension can be clarified on the basis of spacetime holisms's assumptions. It is true that fully describable parts cannot be influenced by phenomena that emerge from their interactions, but there is something wrong with the assumption that there are fully describable and deterministic parts. If we accept the incompleteness of every description, top-down causation becomes much less miraculous. Indeed, most of social science is far away from believing that individuals could in principle be fully described as functional parts. (It is yet another question where we believe the source of non-determinism lies - for spacetime holism, it stems from the fault inherent in any division and not from some inner property.)

2.5 Overlapping Systems – a Road to Holism

As has already become clear from the discussion so far, spacetime holism gives a secondary status to the concept of a system. The system must be understood as a mixture of aspects that, if taken as absolute, contradict each other. In addition to this, being a system is not an objective property. Instead, the question what to treat as a system highly depends on the observer and the level of abstraction. From different views there may appear different systems, which do not at all have to form a hierarchy.

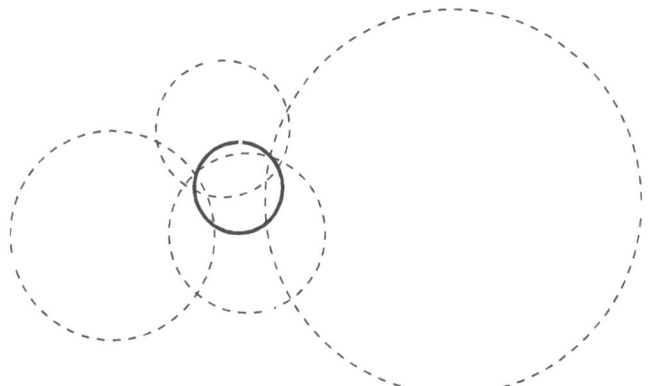

Fig. 2.2. Overlapping systems.

---

[38] (Haken, 1971)

Fig. 2.2 shows schematically what I mean by overlapping systems. Each circle represents a system as it appears to some observer from her or his perspective.

Especially for reductionism, but also for the usual understanding of the theory of self-organization, overlapping systems are forbidden: Either something is a system or it is not.

However, arguing for the necessity to accept overlapping systems is easy (and has already started in section 2.2). Maybe, the best example is the highly interdisciplinary field of cognitive science, where people from most different disciplines throw their views upon one-and-the-same thing, namely biological cognition. By doing so, they talk about systems. What from one perspective is part of the system, belongs to the environment from another perspective. When, e.g. cognition is studied as the product of a social system, the social environment of an individual belongs to the system, whereas the study of cognition as the product of a bunch of brain cells locates other brains in the system's environment. For the social approach to cognition, parts of the nervous system that are not concerned with e.g. language and memory are located in the system's environment.

As long as only hierarchical system relations are allowed, at least one of the two views must be wrong. The consequence for the possibility of interdisciplinary understanding and mutual respect, of course, would be devastating. It would be a mere matter of politeness to listen what people from other disciplines have to say from their – in principle incompatible - viewpoint.

Even when two different views and the systems they deal with are not overlapping, nobody thinks nowadays that either the two views are reducible one to the other or that at least one of them is simply wrong. However, the common sense about the usefulness of most different scientific approaches and descriptions needs a basis which is provided neither by reductionism nor by the theory of self-organization. I dare to say that only a holistic worldview has the potential to give such a basis. Spacetime holism, e.g. by formulating its concepts of duality, tries to overcome the accusation of arbitrariness, which is a typical reaction whenever holistic ideas are uttered.[39]

As has already been addressed in the context of emergence, spacetime holism can accept the bi-directional causation between system levels, as long as the fundamental fault inherent in any division is seen, i.e. as long as no ontological claims are raised for the involved descriptions. When applying this part-whole relation to an infinity of overlapping systems, the infinite complexity of each part can be concluded.

The argument goes as follows: A part both co-produces the whole it belongs to and is influenced by it. This statement requires a certain complexity of the part's behavior – the part must be able to discriminate at least some of the system's states and react to them differently. In a scenario which is

---

[39] E.g. (Fodor & Lepore, 1992).

best described by overlapping systems, a part in the intersection area co-produces two system wholes, by which it is also influenced. This part's behavior must reflect the complexity of both systems, therefore. With each system context the required complexity of the part increases. In addition, the part will also inherit the complexity of all the systems belonging to a possible chain of overlapping systems.

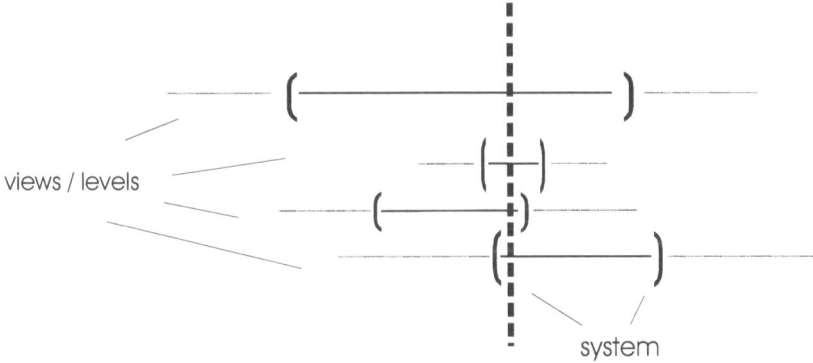

Fig. 2.3. The spectrum of system contexts for one part.

Fig. 2.3 shows one part in the context of a variety of overlapping systems. Only a holistic worldview can explain how this part can usefully be described as a co-producer and product of all these systems.

To turn things around, the holistic consequence of the assumption of overlapping systems might be the reason why usually systems only come in hierarchies, even in the theory of self-organization. When looking at the huge variety of different systems, though, which are very fruitfully being regarded as self-organizing systems, and putting them together in one picture, the existence of overlaps can hardly be denied.

2.6 Part-Whole Containment in Dynamical Systems

The lack of an explicit assumption of part-whole containment in the theory of self-organization has already been criticized. However, there is an argument from dynamical systems theory which sheds a different light on the relation between part-whole containment and the theory of self-organization.

2.6.1 An Intuitive Introduction to Embedding

In this section I will give and intuitive introduction to the idea of *embedding* in dynamical systems theory.[40]

---

[40] (Takens, 1981).

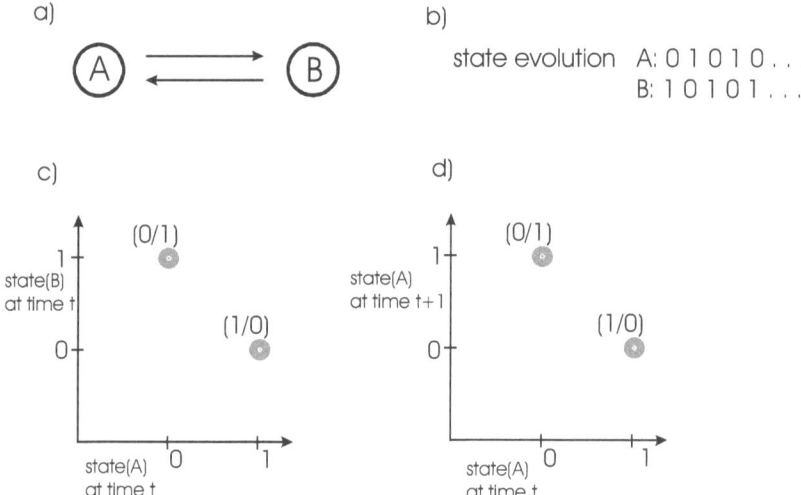

Fig. 2.4. A simple dynamical system. a) units A and B interacting with each other, b) the state evolution in A and B, c) the spatial description of the whole system, d) the temporal description of unit A.

Fig. 2.4a shows a dynamical system consisting of two binary units A and B interacting with each other. If unit A receives 1 (respectively 0) as input from unit B, its next output will be 1 (respectively. 0), the same for unit B. With differing initial values for A and B the whole system will oscillate between 1 and 0 with at each point in time differing states in A and B (Fig. 2.4b). A description of the system behavior in the state space shows two points, namely one for the system state 1/0 (unit A in state 1, unit B in state 0) and one for the system state 0/1 (Fig. 2.4c). This is a mapping of the whole system state at single points in time. We have yet another description - we can map the state evolution for unit A alone. In our example we do this in a two-dimensional coordinate system with A´s state at time t as x-axis and A´s state at time t+1 as y-axis (Fig. 2.4d). Again, we have two points as a result. The point 1/0 means now that when unit A is in the state 1 at time t, it will be in the state 0 at time t+1.

What do we learn from this example? There are two descriptions of the system dynamics, each yielding the same structure. The *temporal description* of a part of the system shows the same structure as the *spatial description* of the whole system. This is, in short, the basic idea of Takens´ theorem of embedding (Takens, 1981) which can be applied also to chaotic dynamics: There are structurally equivalent temporal descriptions for chaotic dynamics that involve only a part of a system. In practice, the extraction of structure from temporal descriptions of different parts will not work equally well. It can be concluded that the infinite structure of a chaotic system is contained in all of its parts (though it cannot be reduced to the stand alone behavior of the parts!). No doubt, the behavior of a part of the system must be seen as produced by the whole system dynamics, yet this part contains the structure of the whole system.

Translated to the language of spacetime holism, embedding in dynamical systems theory means conservation of the omnipresent spacetime structure. The equality of the (spatially large scale - temporally small scale) structure of the spatial description with the (spatially small scale / temporally large scale) structure of the temporal description reflects the two fundamental dualities between space and time and between levels.

It will be shown in the following section how the idea of embedding applies to chaotic dynamics, and what the consequences are for dealing with such infinite structure systems. Before this, I would like to make a remark on fixed point attractor systems like most neural networks. When we reduce our analysis of a dynamical system to the final static states and ask for the relation between the states of single units and the global state (-vector), there is seemingly no significant relation left between part and whole. While it is correct that the state of the part does not reflect the state of the whole, the theorem of embedding still works: The fact that there is only one global state of the system is perfectly mapped to the fact that the state of each single part stays the same for all times.

This all points to the importance of the dynamics (or processuality) of a system, which Bohm has already underlined. It is the spacetime structure that counts, the spatial properties alone do not necessarily show the part-whole relation (fractal structures, of course, do).

2.6.2 Understanding Chaotic Dynamics

The theorem of embedding has a practical application to chaotic systems, which are interesting for spacetime holism due to their infinite complexity. The following procedure[41] is used to forecast chaotic dynamics. In addition, it can be used as a tool for understanding chaotic dynamics in the context of spacetime holism, and especially in the context of overlapping systems.

The only input to the forecasting procedure is a long time series of values of a single variable (or, more generally, a single observable) of a dynamical system. This time series is analyzed, and typical "rules" are extracted. E.g. if the value of the observable took the consecutive values 1-0-1-1-0, then the probability is 63% that the next values will be 1-1-0. (Of course, in this version of the prediction method time as well as space is made discrete: values are taken at fixed time intervals and are mapped to discrete states 0 or 1.) There can be lots of rules with different lengths, and rules may contradict each other in a given situation. After the phase of rule extraction the set of rules can be used to forecast the near future of the observable on the basis of its actual past states. The best

---

[41] In fact, the following is an intuitive illustration of a mixture of methods all based on Taken's theorem of embedding.

matching rule is selected and makes the prediction. One can also think of compromises between matching rules and other variations (e.g. using different granularities of space and time for rule extraction). In this context, however, I am not interested in technical details, but in the general principle.

Another intuitive idea supporting the presented picture of chaotic dynamics is the following: A chaotic attractor can be viewed as an infinite set of competing regular attractors[42] (e.g. oscillations with different frequencies). These partial attractors do not form a hierarchy as is the case in quasi-periodic attractors, which exhibit the shape of so-called *tori* in phase space.

What can be learned from this prediction method for chaotic dynamics is the following. The state evolution of a single observable of a chaotic system, which (at least in the case of deterministic chaos) is a causal product of all the variables of the system, can be understood as a product of the interaction of spatially local "time entities" (i.e. the extracted rules) as well. The usefulness of rules of different types and lengths can be interpreted as the temporal counterpart of the usefulness of the assumption of overlapping systems.

2.6.3 Limitation of Dynamical Systems Theory

Behind most of dynamical systems theory stands the idea that a system's behavior can (at least in principle) be fully described by a set of differential equations. This, of course, gives a secondary status to the time entities that are the basis of the above introduced prediction method. However, a closer look at differential equations shows that they still represent the traditional understanding of space and time, namely that there are identifyable entities in space (the variables in state space) and that time is continuous. These two assumptions combine to the idea that everything can be described by trajectories, which means in the language of spacetime holism that a fundamental level of particle-like description is assumed.

Chaos theory, therefore, cannot be accepted as a fully satisfying account of spacetime holism. What misses is the equal status for wave and particle aspects. However, chaos theory seems to mark the border line between the traditional worldview and spacetime holism. Still on the basis of the concept of the trajectory, chaotic dynamics show infinite and overlapping structure in space and time, they show sometimes fractal structure, and they show spacetime holism's duality relations.

2.7 Summary

It has been shown how the theory of self-organization can be founded in spacetime holism and how the problems centering around the notions of causality and emergence are resolved by this move. Instead of exactly defining the concept of a system (which is impossible in spacetime holism), it has

---

[42] (Diito&Pecora, 1993)

been suggested to understand the system as a mixture of competing aspects, which are related to spacetime holism's structural notions.

In order to deal with the impossibility of defining perfect system hierarchies, the notion of "overlapping systems" has been suggested, which, together with the concept of embedding from dynamical systems theory, will allow to formulate spacetime holism's account of representation.

3 Spacetime and Relativity Theory

Contribution to the Thesis

In support of the worldview of spacetime holism, it is shown that the integrated view of space and time matches with relativity theory. On the basis of a clear treatment of spacetime holism's distinction between inside and outside observation, a new interpretation of relativity theory is formulated, which makes an intuitive understanding of spacetime in terms of a Euclidean geometry possible. This interpretation makes also use of systems theoretical concepts, which have already been founded in spacetime holism.

3.1 Introduction

One of spacetime holism's central features is the full integration of space and time to spacetime. At first sight, this seems to be exactly what special and general relativity tell us. However, a closer look at how this unification of space and time is achieved in the standard interpretation of relativity theory reveals that the so-called spacetime continuum does not provide an intuitive interface (not even to the physicist) for more general theorizing about spacetime. Yet, this is what spacetime holism is all about, namely a set of coherent assumptions and views that are applicable in a wide range of domains.

In this chapter I will show that special relativity with its formalism and its experimental confirmation does allow a different interpretation – one that is not only simpler to understand and apply, but that also overcomes a tricky philosophical problem connected with the standard interpretation. The *normalization problem of special relativity* is due to an unclear treatment of the distinction between inside and outside concepts of observation.

In the first section I discuss the normalization problem of special relativity and thereby develop an alternative derivation of the Lorentz transformations, which are the essence of special relativity. After this, I will introduce the alternative interpretation of special relativity, which is called *Euclidean interpretation*, in more detail and in a wider context. The last section of this chapter deals with a perspective for a new approach to general relativity on the basis of the Euclidean interpretation.

3.2 The Normalization Problem of Special Relativity[43]

The following investigation into the meaning of special relativity starts from the question how observers in relative motion may achieve an agreement on their space and time scales. As this *normalization problem* does not receive a thorough treatment in Einstein's development of the

---

[43] The arguments presented in this section have been published in (Winkler, 2002b).

Lorentz transformations, two possible solutions are discussed in the framework of special relativity. They will be called *normalization at rest* and *normalization in motion*. It will be shown that these solutions are related to different interpretations of the Lorentz transformations. In the case of normalization in motion, the Lorentz transformations can be developed by the exclusive use of conventions; in fact, the relativity principle and the principle of the invariance of the speed of light would play the role of mere conventions for a solution to the normalization problem. Normalization at rest requires an assumption concerning the acceleration of objects. It is shown that an adequate assumption can replace the relativity principle in the derivation of the Lorentz transformations.

Neither normalization in motion nor normalization at rest seem to be compatible with the standard interpretation of special relativity. Therefore, an alternative interpretation of special relativity not only deviating from the standard interpretation, but also from Lorentz-type interpretations is suggested. It is based on the analysis of the normalization problem and on the conceptual distinction between *inside* and *outside* observation already introduced in section 1.3.

3.2.1 The Normalization Problem

To measure means to compare. In hard science, the conditions under which a measurement takes place have to be defined very strictly. Most importantly, it has to be assured that the measuring instruments, i.e. the tools with which the investigated phenomena are compared, are in a well-defined sense the *same* for every measurement. Only when this is guaranteed to a certain extent, it is justified to relate the measured phenomena to each other.

Out of these basic considerations about the measurement procedure a question arises for the special theory of relativity, which deals with measurements stemming from observers in relative motion: By which procedure do different observers (inertial frames of reference) assure that their measuring instruments are the same, and, consequently, in which sense can space and time scales held by different observers be considered the same?

This question will be analyzed as the *normalization problem of special relativity*. In Einstein's development of the relativistic calculus, the normalization problem is not addressed. It is, though, a problem that has to be solved whenever measurements stemming from different observers are related to each other as is done in the Lorentz transformations.

In order to make the role of the normalization problem for the special theory of relativity and the implications for its interpretation explicit, two possible solutions to the normalization problem will be discussed, which will be called *normalization at rest* and *normalization in motion*.

3.2.1.1 Normalization at Rest

The most natural way to solve the normalization problem is to build two identical sets of measuring instruments (meter sticks and clocks) that rest in a first frame of reference and transfer one of them to a second, moving frame. After that the measuring instruments of the second frame can be adapted to the first frame. This procedure requires the acceleration of a set of measuring instruments.

Though avoiding the term acceleration, Einstein seems to have normalization at rest in mind when introducing the relativity of lengths (Einstein, 1905). In his scenario, only one meter stick is used, yet in two different (constant) states of motion. At first, the meter stick and some object rest in frame 1. The length of the object is measured by the meter stick. Then the same meter stick and the same object appear as resting in another frame 2 showing some constant motion relative to frame 1. Again, a measurement of the object takes place by the use of the meter stick. According to the relativity principle, it is postulated that both measurements must yield the same value for the length of the object. As a consequence, it turns out that both meter stick and object resting in frame 2 show a contraction when being measured in frame 1 (and vice versa).

In the case of normalization at rest, the space and time scales of different frames are adapted with the help of an accelerated set of measuring instruments. By this, the identity of the scales of different frames is directly given. In the case of normalization in motion, such direct adaptation is impossible.

3.2.1.2 Normalization in Motion

As normalization at rest is linked to the acceleration of objects, it should not be the choice of the proponents of the standard interpretation, who regard length contraction and time dilation as properties of spacetime as such. As an adequate basis of this view, a different class of normalization procedures can be introduced, which will be called *normalization in motion*. The basic idea of normalization in motion is that two observers aiming at an agreement on meters and seconds stay in constant relative motion when performing the normalization procedure.

In the following, three versions of normalization in motion are offered, all of which are based on the relativity principle. Two observers solving their normalization problem in relative motion choose their scales of space and time such that the relativity principle is satisfied.

Normalization by Postulated Identity (I). It is usually taken as an empirical fact that certain physical objects or processes have identical spatial or temporal extensions from the view of their rest frames. Good examples are decay processes of atoms producing radiation of some fixed wavelength. Yet, as long as observers in different states of motion performing an experiment have not come to an agreement on meters and seconds, this extensional identity can only be a postulate. This postulate, however, could be interpreted as an instruction for different observers to solve their normalization problem, namely in the following sense: Every observer has to choose the length of his meter stick such that the selected process has the postulated extension. By this, the relativity principle is satisfied, as the measured extensions depend exclusively on the relative speed with respect to the observer. (The relative speed equals zero in this trivial case.)

Normalization by the Use of a Moving Object (II). As will be shown in section 3.2.2, the normalization problem need not be solved in order to allow different observers to perform useful and compatible measurements of velocities. On this basis, any two non-normalized observers in relative constant motion may arrange a scenario, in which an object moves with some velocity v from the view of the first observer and with the velocity $-v$ from the view of the second observer. According to the relativity principle, both observers should measure the length of the object to the same value. Again, two observers could take this assertion as a basis for the normalization of their meter sticks.

Normalization by mutual measurement (III). The minimal construction involves only two observers agreeing on their relative motion. Other than procedure (II), which requires a referential object resting in a third frame, procedure (III) is based on mutual measurements of meter sticks resting in the frames that are to be adapted. The involved observers vary the lengths of their (arbitrarily chosen) meter sticks until they measure each other's meter sticks to the same value. This solution, like the previous one, presupposes compatible measurements of velocities by non-normalized observers.

Though all three solutions to the normalization problem are built upon the relativity principle, they are not equivalent from a philosophical point of view. Solution (I) requires the assumption that there are copies of physical objects or processes which can be treated the same in different states of motion by co-moving observers. Solutions (II) and (III) do not use copies. The clarification of this difference requires a closer look at the relativity principle.

The relativity principle postulates that the *form* of the laws of physics is the same in all inertial frames. Using the relativity principle as a basis for a solution to the normalization problem - to be precise - goes beyond that meaning, insofar as the form of a law has nothing to do with the scaling of the measured variables.

How can two observers not yet having solved their normalization problem conclude that they have to do with the same objects or processes when performing some experiment in their rest frames? All they can do is to compare the set of relations between the variables they measured in their own experiment with the set of relations between the variables measured by the other observer in his experiment. If the relations are equivalent, then it is justified to assume that the same *types* of objects or processes were involved in both experiments. However, it is not legitimate to conclude that also the extensions must be identical. Formal equivalence does not imply equivalence with respect to scaling. Only by an act of definition, i.e. by setting the scales accordingly (normalization procedure (I)), are the extensions of the two objects or processes made identical.

Normalization in relative motion, irrespective of the chosen procedure, is a legitimate option, as the relativity principle is available in the axiomatic system leading to the Lorentz transformations. However, the implications for the interpretation of the Lorentz transformations are enormous. If the normalization problem is solved at relative rest by the use of accelerated measuring instruments, the validity of the Lorentz transformations is an empirical question: Is it true that an accelerated meter stick shows the expected contraction? If, instead, the relativity principle comes in as a *convention* for the normalization of measuring instruments resting in inertial frames, the validity of the Lorentz transformations is tautological. This difference will be demonstrated in a thought experiment in section 3.2.5.

3.2.2 Coordinate Transformations for Non-Normalized Observers

There are many different ways to derive the Lorentz transformations (e.g. Alexandrow, 1996; Ehrlichson, 1973), all of which ignore the normalization problem. In the following, a development of the Lorentz transformations is suggested that makes the treatment of the normalization problem explicit. As a first step, a set of coordinate transformations is introduced that leaves the normalization problem still open. In section 3.2.3 it is shown how normalization in motion leads to the Lorentz transformations, in section 3.2.4 the same is shown for normalization at rest.

3.2.2.1 Spacetime Frames

The presented approach to special relativity makes use of a fully Euclidean spacetime geometry. The central concept of a spacetime frame and its relation to measurements of space and time distances can be characterized as follows.

Measurements and spacetime frames. *On the one hand a spacetime frame has to be regarded as a geometrical construction on the basis of measurements of space and time distances performed by an observer, on the other hand every spacetime frame can be used to describe the measurement processes performed by observers in relative motion. It is thus possible for every observer holding a frame to reconstruct the frames held by observers in relative motion by measuring their measuring processes.*

As a consequence of this, special relativity can be developed from the perspective of any single frame. The equivalence of all inertial frames is a logical consequence of the validity of the Lorentz transformations, which can be derived in the Euclidean spacetime geometry of a single observer. Before this is done, some remarks on the following argumentation have to be made.

For the purpose of this thesis, it is sufficient to deal with only one space dimension in addition to the time dimension.[44] The orthogonality of the space and time axes is nothing more than a convenient choice making geometrical relations and calculations easy. There is no physical argument forcing the mapping of pairs of measured space and time distances between events to a rectangular geometry. In the diagrams, the time axis is scaled with the constant c (speed of light), which makes light rays appear as 45° lines.

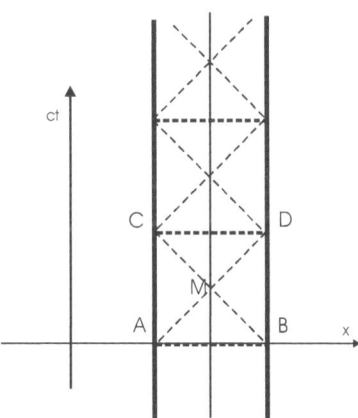

Fig. 3.1. A resting light clock consisting of two mirrors between which two light rays are reflected. The light rays meet in the middle point M. Events A and B respectively C and D are simultaneous.

In Fig. 3.1 the concept of a light clock is introduced in the framework of an observer, for whom the invariance of the speed of light is assumed. In addition to Einstein's light clock a second light ray is reflected between two mirrors, which are fastened at the end points of a stick. The light rays are synchronized such that they always meet in the middle point M of the stick. By this, Einstein's definition of synchrony holds for events A and B as well as for events C and D.

While Fig. 3.1 shows a resting light clock, the light clock of Fig. 3.2 is in motion along the x-axis. For the moving clock, the events A' and B' as well as the events C' and D' are synchronous. The associated space and time axes of the moving clock show an angle γ relative to the axes of the rest frame.

---

[44] Thus, the normalization problem is considered only for meter sticks showing the same spatial orientation. A more complete coverage of the normalization problem would comprise the adaptation of meter sticks with different spatial orientations. Similar to the normalization problem for moving meter sticks in one dimension, there is a *conventional option*, which is based on the conventional constancy of the speed of light in all directions, and a *non-conventional option*, which is based on the rotation of a meter stick.

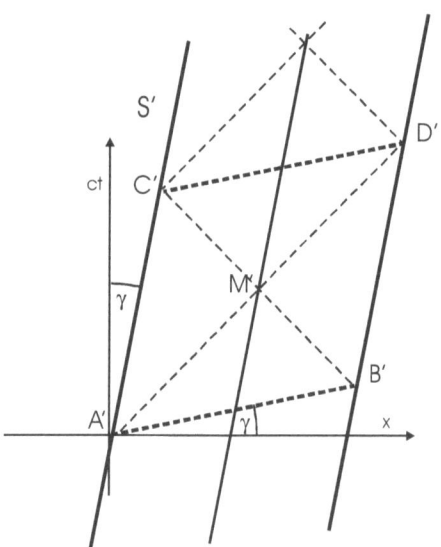

Fig. 3.2. A moving light clock. Events A' and B' respectively events C' and D' are simultaneous.

The clocks in Fig. 3.1 and Fig. 3.2 represent inertial observers holding their own spacetime frames. The parallelograms *ABCD* respectively *A'B'C'D'* can be regarded as the elementary cells of these frames, which hold spacetime coordinates for all possible events, including all events belonging to the measurement procedures performed by different observers.

The assumption that light has an invariant speed for both observers can very easily be implemented by the following convention.[45]

Conventional invariance of the speed of light. In order to make the speed of light invariant in all inertial frames, each observer takes the arbitrarily chosen length of his light clock to be 1 meter and the temporal interval between two reflections ("ticks") as 1 second divided by c. If all observers do so, the speed of light is fixed to c. From now on, it is assumed that for all inertial observers – by this *convention* – the speed of light is c.

Before showing how frames can be mapped to each other, the mutual measurements of two observers are illustrated by the use of the light clocks that represent their frames. Fig. 3.3 shows two observers (light clocks) in relative motion who take the length of their own stick to be *1 meter*. The simultaneous measurement of the other observer's stick marks a Euclidean spacetime distance that

---

[45] Note that the assumption of the invariance of the speed of light (for all inertial observers) presupposes a solution to the normalization problem. As long as the normalization problem is not solved, the invariance of the speed of light cannot be an empirical fact, but only a convention.

is compared to the meter stick of the observer performing the measurement. For *S'* the length of *S* is *x'* divided by *1 meter(S')*. For *S* the length of *S'* is *x* divided by *1 meter(S)*.

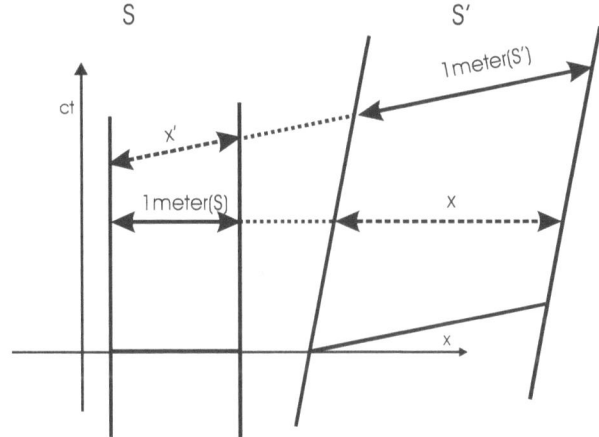

Fig. 3.3. Two observers measure each other's lengths simultaneously from their own point of view.

3.2.2.2 Derivation of the Transformations for Space and Time Distances

The transformations of space and time distances held by a resting frame *S* to a frame *S'* moving with velocity *v* can be derived using Fig. 3.4.

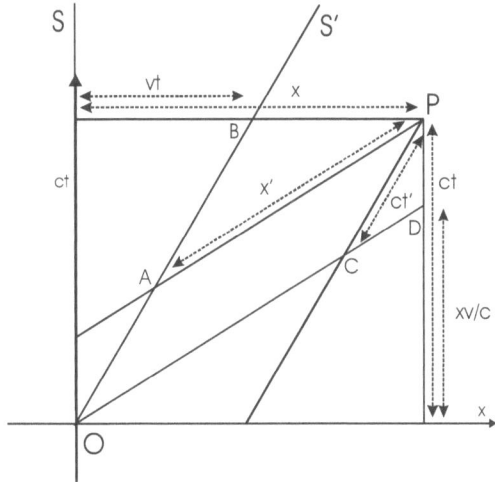

Fig. 3.4. The coordinates of event *P* are measured in the resting frame *S* and in the frame *S'* which moves with velocity *v* relative to *S*. Both coordinate systems are assumed to have the same origin *O*. The similarity of the triangles *ABP* and *CDP* allows to formulate the transformations for space and time distances from frame *S* to frame *S'*.

The two non-normalized frames in Fig. 3.4 have a common origin in event O. In both frames the space and time coordinates of event P are measured. The diagram shows the perspective of frame S, whose time axis is scaled with c. However, the following arguments hold for the perspective of any inertial observer. As has already been shown in Fig. 3.2, in such illustrations the space and time axes of frame S' have the same angle relative to the axis of the resting frame S. From this it follows that the triangles ABP and CDP are similar, which allows to formulate the following relation.

$$N = \frac{x'}{x - v \cdot t} = \frac{c \cdot t'}{c \cdot t - \frac{v \cdot x}{c}}$$

(3.1)

The term N plays a key role for the normalization problem; therefore it will be called *normalization term*. As a consequence of (3.1), the transformations for space and time distances from frame S to frame S' take the form:

$$T(S => S')$$
$$\Delta x' = N \cdot (\Delta x - v \cdot \Delta t)$$
$$\Delta t' = N \cdot (\Delta t - \frac{v \cdot \Delta x}{c^2})$$

(3.2)

The normalization term N is responsible for the scaling of the resulting space and time distances in S'. For each choice of the length of the meter stick in S' there is a corresponding value for N. It will be shown that the selection of a value for the normalization term N of a set of transformations T (S=>S') determines the value N^{-1} of the inverse transformations T^{-1}(S'=>S).

Before clarifying the relation between N and N^{-1}, three important properties of the transformations between in general not normalized observers have to be listed:

(a) There is one signal whose speed is invariant for all observers. This is already given by the way the spacetime frames of inertial observers are constructed. For this construction, the invariance of the speed of light is a mere convention. In section 3.2.5, the assumption of an invariant signal other than light will be discussed.

(b) Two observers agree on their relative velocity. The validity of this statement can easily be demonstrated by describing the world line of a point resting in frame S and by transferring it to the frame S', which moves relative to S with speed v.

$$\Delta x = 0 \cdot \Delta t$$
$$\Delta x' = N \cdot (0 - v \cdot \Delta t)$$
$$\Delta t' = N \cdot (\Delta t - \frac{v \cdot 0}{c^2})$$
$$v' = \frac{\Delta x'}{\Delta t'} = -v$$
(3.3)

Independent of the (non-zero) value of N, the speed of the frame S from the view of S' is $-v$.

(c) The relativistic addition theorem for velocities holds. The derivation of the addition theorem for velocities is essentially the same as when using the Lorentz transformations. In inertial frame S a point moves with constant speed v_1. The coordinates of that point are described from the view of a system S' that moves relative to S with speed $-v_2$. After that, the speed v of the point from the view of S' is calculated.

$$\Delta x = v_1 \cdot \Delta t$$
$$\Delta x' = N \cdot (\Delta x + v_2 \cdot \Delta t) = N \cdot (v_1 \cdot \Delta t + v_2 \cdot \Delta t)$$
$$\Delta t' = N \cdot (\Delta t + \frac{v_2 \cdot \Delta x}{c^2}) = N \cdot (\Delta t + \frac{v_1 \cdot v_2 \cdot \Delta t}{c^2})$$
$$v_1 \oplus v_2 = v = \frac{\Delta x'}{\Delta t'} = \frac{v_1 + v_2}{1 + \frac{v_1 \cdot v_2}{c^2}}$$
(3.4)

Also in this calculation, the value of N is irrelevant for the resulting velocity v. Once more it should be stressed that the statements (b) and (c) concerning velocities do not depend on a solution to the normalization problem. They also do not depend on the relativity principle. In the suggested Euclidean spacetime geometry, they are derived from the definition of the measurement procedures (including the definition of synchrony) and the convention of the invariance of the speed of light.

3.2.2.3 The relation between two normalization terms

For the transformations $T(S=>S')$ and for the inverse transformations $T^{-1}(S'=>S)$ between two frames in relative motion, a change of the length of a meter stick in one frame always has an effect on both normalization terms. The relation between N and N^{-1} can be calculated by assuming that a spacetime interval as being measured by frame S is mapped to itself when first being transformed to frame S' and afterwards being re-transformed to frame S.

$T(S => S')$

$$\Delta x' = N \cdot (\Delta x - v \cdot \Delta t)$$

$$\Delta t' = N \cdot (\Delta t - \frac{v \cdot \Delta x}{c^2})$$

$T^{-1}(S' => S)$

$$\Delta x = N^{-1} \cdot (\Delta x' + v \cdot \Delta t')$$

$$\Delta t = N^{-1} \cdot (\Delta t' + \frac{v \cdot \Delta x'}{c^2})$$

This leads straightforward to

$$N \cdot N^{-1} = \frac{1}{1 - \frac{v^2}{c^2}}$$

(3.5)

As a consequence of both normalization in motion and normalization at rest, the values for N and N^{-1} will be shown to be equal, which leads to the Lorentz transformations. However, different and as well consistent[46] choices for N and N^{-1} are possible. E.g., a scenario can be imagined, in which all frames S' adapt their meter sticks such that the meter stick of a selected frame S is measured by them to 1 meter. Accordingly, the frames S' would measure also time intervals to the same values as frame S. Applying (2) and (5) leads to the normalization terms for this scenario.

$$N = \frac{1}{1 - \frac{v^2}{c^2}} \qquad N^{-1} = 1$$

(3.6)

3.2.3 Normalization by the Relativity Principle

The transformations T describe the mapping of space and time distances between inertial frames that have not solved their normalization problem, i.e. the lengths of the meter sticks have been chosen independently. The term N is responsible for the scaling of both space and time distances in S'. Procedures fixing the terms N and N^{-1} for the transformations between two frames and consequently the lengths of the observers' meter sticks are normalization procedures. One such normalization procedure follows from the relativity principle, saying: "Two inertial observers choose the lengths of their meter sticks such that they measure each other's meter stick to the same value." This normalization procedure has already been introduced as *normalization by mutual measurement* (III). In order to make the velocity of light equal c also after the normalization, the time scales have to be re-adapted.

---

[46] The consistency of such alternatives is limited to 1-dimensional space. The integration of a second or third spatial dimension is not compatible with the constancy of the speed of light for all spatial directions.

In the following calculation of the normalization terms for the transformations between two frames S and S', the length of the meter stick of frame S as measured by frame S' is regarded as the result of the transformation of the spacetime interval, which describes the length measurement of the meter stick of S performed by S', from S to S'.

$len'(meter(S))$...length of the meter stick of S from the view of S'

$$len'(meter(S)) = N \cdot (1 - \frac{v^2}{c^2}) \qquad (3.7)$$

Applying (3.6) leads to

$$len'(meter(S)) = \frac{1}{N^{-1}} \qquad (3.8)$$

The same procedure leads to the length of the meter stick of S' from the view of S.

$$len(meter(S')) = \frac{1}{N} \qquad (3.9)$$

According to normalization procedure (III), the mutual measurements of the meter sticks must yield the same result.

$$len'(meter(S)) = len(meter(S')) \qquad (3.10)$$

Therefore the two normalization terms N and N^1 must be identical, which allows to calculate their value.

$$N = N^{-1} = \frac{1}{\sqrt{1 - \frac{v^2}{c^2}}} \qquad (3.11)$$

Inserting this expression for N to the formulae of the transformations T leads to the Lorentz transformations. This step completes a derivation of the Lorentz transformations which solves the normalization problem in relative motion by the use of the relativity principle.

However, this solution has a disadvantage which is connected to the interpretation of special relativity: Length contraction and time dilation are mere consequences of conventions, namely the constancy of the speed of light and the relativity principle, which stand behind normalization in motion. There is no possibility to conclude from this that an object which at first rests in one frame and then accelerates until it rests in the other frame shows the relativistic length contraction. Yet, this statement is part of the interpretation of special relativity as it stands.

In order to provide the full meaning of length contraction, an assumption on acceleration is inescapable and - as will be shown - sufficient.

3.2.4 Normalization by an Assumption on Acceleration

Solving the normalization problem at rest requires an assumption on acceleration. In this section, an assumption is formulated which is motivated by Einstein's treatment of length contraction. The approach will be discussed in section 3.2.4.3.

3.2.4.1 Identity and Acceleration

The scenario in which Einstein introduces the contraction of lengths consists of two measurements yielding the same value for the length of an object: At first, the object and the meter stick rest in some inertial frame, after that, both the meter stick and the measured object are in the same state of constant motion relative to the original rest frame. The identity of the measured lengths might be explained by a simple assumption on acceleration, which is not made explicit by Einstein, though.

Hidden Assumption on Accelerating Objects. Accelerating objects stay identical from their own perspective.

In order to make this assumption exploitable for mathematical analysis, the perspective of the accelerating object has to be defined. This can be done by the use of *tangent frames*.[47]

Tangent Frame. A tangent frame is an inertial frame from whose perspective a continuously accelerating object rests for a point in time.

In the infinitesimal limit, the velocities shortly before and shortly after this point in time take the same value for the tangent frame, differing only in direction.[48] It is therefore possible to regard the tangent frame as a kind of reflector for accelerating objects. Each continuous acceleration can be constructed from an infinity of infinitesimally small reflections or *"sudden changes"*.

Once the perspective of the accelerating object is defined as the perspective of the actual tangent frame, an assumption on acceleration can be formulated that supports Einstein's hidden assumption.

Assumption of Simultaneous Change. A change of the velocity of an object takes place simultaneously for the object.

On the basis of this assumption it will be shown in section 3.2.4.2 that any discrete sudden change of the velocity of an object leads to the Lorentz contraction and consequently to the relativistic normalization term N. The validity of this also for the limiting case of continuous acceleration is a mathematical consequence.

---

[47] The concept of a tangent frame has been introduced by Einstein (1916) and is common in general relativity.
48 This holds whenever the second derivative of the object's world line exists.

3.2.4.2 Derivation of the Normalization Term by the Assumption of Simultaneous Change

The assumption of simultaneous change allows to derive the normalization term N and thereby solves the normalization problem.

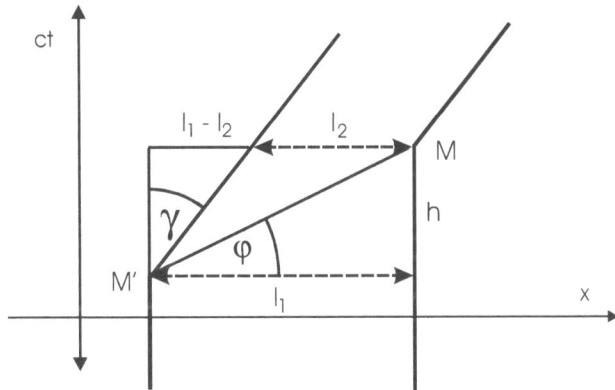

Fig. 3.5. The distance l_1 between two resting points changes to l_2, when they "suddenly" accelerate to the same velocity, but at different points in time. The events E and E' are simultaneous for the tangent frame, whose space axis shows an angle φ relative to the resting frame's space axis. The time axis of the points after the sudden change show an angle γ relative to the time axis of the resting frame.

Fig. 3.5 shows the world lines of two resting points that suddenly change their velocity to v. They do so at events E and E' which are simultaneous from the view of some tangent frame moving with speed v_T. Equations (3.12) and (3.13) express the geometrical relations of the diagram.

$$\tan \gamma = \frac{v}{c} = \frac{l_1 - l_2}{h} \tag{3.12}$$

$$\tan \varphi = \frac{v_T}{c} = \frac{h}{l_1} \tag{3.13}$$

The fact that v_T is the velocity of the tangent frame can be expressed by applying the addition theorem, which has already been derived for the transformations T between non-normalized inertial frames (4).

$$v = v_T \oplus v_T = \frac{2 \cdot v_T}{1 + \frac{v_T^2}{c^2}} \tag{3.14}$$

From these equations the contraction term K and consequently the normalization term N^{-1} of the inverse transformations can be calculated.[49]

$$K = \frac{l_2}{l_1} = \sqrt{1 - \frac{v^2}{c^2}} \qquad (3.15)$$

$$N^{-1} = \frac{1}{K} = \frac{1}{\sqrt{1 - \frac{v^2}{c^2}}} \qquad (3.16)$$

Once the normalization term N^{-1} of the inverse transformations takes this value, the normalization term N must be identical according to (3.5).

$$N = \frac{1}{\sqrt{1 - \frac{v^2}{c^2}}} \qquad (3.17)$$

3.2.4.3 Discussion of the Assumption of Simultaneous Change

The assumption of simultaneous change leads to an accelerating behavior of extended physical objects which is known as *Fermi-Walker transport*.[50] It is connected with the concepts *rigid object* and *rigid motion of objects*.[51] Other than in the literature, where rigid motion is introduced by infinitesimal Lorentz transformations, it has been shown in this section that rigid motion, as an implementation of normalization at rest, allows a non-conventional derivation of the Lorentz transformations.

Building the Lorentz transformations upon the assumption of rigid objects creates a strange situation: Rigidity is not compatible with special relativity's limitation of physical effects to the speed of light. A rigid objects reacts "as a whole" when being accelerated, whereas from a classical, atomistic point of view such behavior is forbidden.

The non-rigid acceleration of physical objects produces tensions,[52] which means that spatial relations between parts of the object, as being measured by the tangent frame, undergo changes.

---

[49] The relation between the contraction term K and the normalization term N^{-1} of the inverse transformations can be read from (3.8).
[50] (Misner et. al., 1973)
[51] (Pauli, 1958)
[52] (Pauli, 1958)

However, this does not imply that the relativistic length relations do not hold after an object's acceleration. It could very well be the case that objects have the ability to restore the correct relativistic lengths after the tensions have come to an end. This would not only require that the object "memorizes" the spatial relations between its parts. It would also be necessary that the correct relativistic length is kept by at least one part, to which the lengths of all other parts could be re-adapted. As a consequence, rigidity has to be postulated at least for parts of physical objects in order to support normalization at rest and thereby the non-conventional meaning of length contraction.

As classical physics does not allow rigidity, it seems natural to seek rigidity and consequently a foundation of special relativity in the domain of quantum mechanics. The existence of non-local phenomena[53] as being postulated by quantum mechanics might provide an appropriate basis for this undertaking.

3.2.5 The Role of the Invariant Signaling Speed

The speed of light plays a key role for the conservation of an object's identity through a process of acceleration: It is the simultaneity on the basis of the *speed of light* which brings forth the right contraction term of the Lorentz transformations. Thereby the definition of synchrony, the invariance of the speed of light, and the relativity principle loose their conventional character.

In the following, it will be shown that the conventional invariance of a speed different from that of light as the basis for the Lorentz transformations is in principle possible. The calculus works perfectly and does not lead to contradictions (e.g. time paradoxes). However, there are strong consequences for the description of acceleration and length contraction, as well as for scenarios involving signals that are faster than the chosen invariant signal.

3.2.5.1 Special Relativity in a Medium

As a thought experiment, the spacetime frames of observers moving in a medium are analyzed who use the speed of sound waves in the medium (c_l) instead of light in the vacuum.[54]

Sound observers use sound clocks instead of light clocks. The spacetime frames of sound observers are constructed in the same way as has been done for light observers: Constantly moving sound observers

- *choose rods of arbitrary lengths as their meter sticks and define the time between two ticks of their sound clocks as one second divided by c_l,*

---

[53] (Einstein, Podolsky, Rosen, 1935)
54 The discussion of a relativity theory based on a different invariant signal than light is inspired by Svozil (2000).

- adapt their meter sticks such that they measure each others meter sticks to the same value (i.e. perform normalization procedure (III)), and

- re-adapt their time scales such that the speed of sound, again, equals c_1.

From the same arguments as in sections 3.2.2 and 3.2.3 it follows that the transformations between two frames take the form:[55]

$$\Delta x' = \frac{(\Delta x - v \cdot \Delta t)}{\sqrt{1 - \frac{v^2}{c_1^2}}} \qquad \Delta t' = \frac{(\Delta t - \frac{v \cdot \Delta x}{c_1^2})}{\sqrt{1 - \frac{v^2}{c_1^2}}} \qquad (3.18)$$

As a consequence of these formulae, the motion of an observer relative to the medium cannot be read from the spacetime measurements based on sound. However, when the readings of co-moving clocks based on different signaling velocities (sound and light) are compared, a difference appears which depends on the motion relative to the medium.

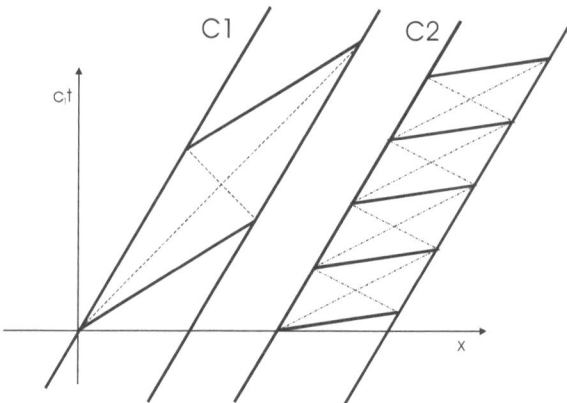

Fig. 3.6. From the rest frame of the medium, the spacetime cells of a sound clock *C1* and a light clock *C2* moving at the same speed are illustrated. Observers using different clocks disagree on which events are simultaneous.

Fig. 3.6 shows two such observers and their differing views of space and time. The observers no longer agree on which spatially separated events are simultaneous. From the view of the rest frame of the medium, the space axis of the sound observer is steeper than the space axis of the light observer. If, instead, both observers were at rest relative to the medium, their space axes would be identical.

---

55 The relative velocity of the frames is limited to c_1.

More serious problems arise when objects are accelerated. The contraction terms of ordinary (light based) special relativity and of sound based special relativity result in different values. The fact that the sound based contraction term will not stand experimental tests shows the mere conventional character of sound relativity. Despite these shortcomings, there are no causal problems for sound relativity. Contrasting Svozil's approach,[56] it will be shown that the use of light signals does not lead to time paradoxes for sound observers.

3.2.5.2 Faster-than-Sound Communication

The following example shows the extreme case of faster-than-sound communication, namely when a signal is used that is "faster than the space axis" of a moving sound frame. In Fig. 3.7 two co-moving sound observers exchange light signals. Observer $O1$ sends a light signal in the direction of observer $O2$ at event A. The signal is received by $O2$ at event B' and immediately answered by a signal directed at $O1$. This signal is received by $O1$ at event C. For the observers $O1$ and $O2$, the events A and A', B and B' as well as C and C' are synchronous.

As can be read from the diagram, the two observers agree on the following statements.

- *The first signal moves backward in time and is received before its emission.* $(A > B')$
- *The second signal moves forward in time and is received after its emission.* $(C > B')$

Although it is possible to send signals "backward in time" in one direction, it is impossible to construct causal paradoxes: No event can ever depend causally on a later event at the same location $(A < C)$.[57]

---

[56] (Svozil, 2000)
57 The example could be used in the discussion around hypothetical tachyons (Recami, 1987). Sound observers detecting light signals are in a similar situation as physicists would be when detecting faster-than-light signaling via tachyons.

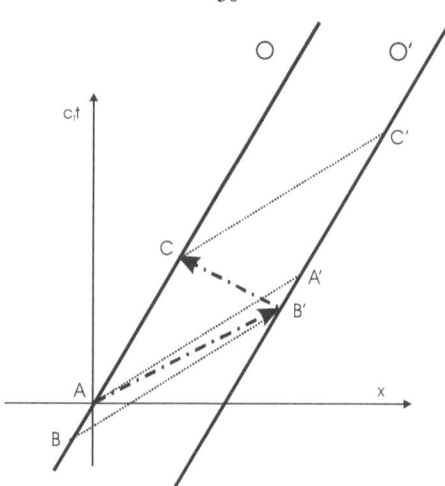

Fig. 3.7. Two sound-observers holding synchronized clocks are moving through the medium. Observer *O1* sends a light signal at event A to observer *O2*. The signal is received at event B' and immediately answered by another light signal which is received by observer *O1* at event C. In one direction, a light signal can destroy the temporal order between emission and reception (A > B), but not in both directions (B < C). Events taking place in one point in space cannot lose their temporal order (A < C). This means that causal paradoxes are not possible.

3.3 The Interpretation of Special Relativity

In this section I will put the rather technical treatment of the normalization problem and the derivation of the Lorentz transformations into perspective. At first, I will show the intuitive gain of the presented approach to special relativity by the use of the famous twin paradox. After that, I will introduce the standard (Minkowski) interpretation as well as Lorentz-type interpretations. The Euclidean interpretation, which is elaborated in more detail and in the context of spacetime holism, significantly differs from both approaches.

3.3.1 The Twin Paradox

Moving clocks go slower. This central statement of special relativity, when being freed from the specific context of application, produces a seeming paradox, which is known as twin or clock paradox.

A couple of twins decides to participate in an experiment to test the special theory of relativity. One of the twins leaves the earth in a very fast moving spaceship in the direction of some distant star. Once having arrived, he turns around and returns home. From the viewpoint of the other twin who stayed on the earth, the travelling twin must have aged less, i.e. he must be younger when the two twins meet again. However, for the travelling twin the "resting" brother is moving, therefore, he should be younger. This, of course, cannot both be true: One twin cannot be younger and older than the other twin at the same time. Consequently, special relativity must be wrong.

In order to get rid of the problems imposed by the twin paradox it is often argued that the scenario must be analyzed in the framework of general relativity, as it involves acceleration and therefore non-linearity. Yet, a linear version of the paradox can be constructed that fully conserves the problem.[58]

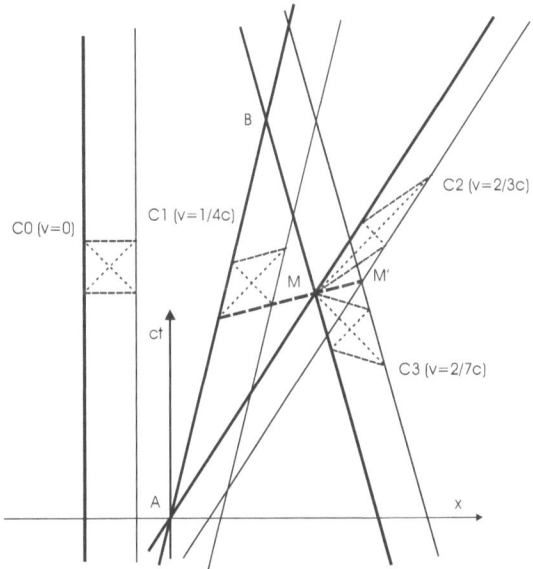

Fig. 3.8. The linear version of the twin paradox from the view of a non-involved observer represented by clock $C0$. The transfer from $C2$ to $C3$ can be read as a sudden change that is simultaneous for $C1$, the "resting" observer.

In a resting frame three identical clocks are built. One of them ($C1$) stays at rest, the others ($C2$ and $C3$) are accelerated to (finally constant) velocities v and $-v$ such that the following scenario becomes possible. The clock $C2$ with velocity v passes by the resting clock $C1$ at event A, at which both clocks are reset. After some time the moving clocks $C2$ and $C3$ meet at event M, at which the state of the clock $C2$ is transferred to $C3$. Finally, $C1$ and $C3$ meet at event B and compare their time counters.

In Fig. 3.8 the whole scenario of the linear twin paradox is illustrated from the view of yet another, not involved frame represented by the clock $C0$. This was done in order to indicate the independence of the assertions from the chosen perspective. For all four perspectives the number of ticks of each clock between two events (e.g. clock $C2$, events A and M) is the same. Although the rate of an observed clock depends on the relative motion between observed clock and observer, the time passed for a clock between two events is objective. From this it follows that all possible

---

[58] E.g. (Brandes, 1995).

observers will come to the same conclusion concerning the age of the twins. Another point of agreement for all observers is the fact that there is a change of velocity for the combined system C2-C3. In accordance with the treatment of his scenario in the standard as well in Lorentz-type interpretations of special relativity, this is the clue to dissolve the twin paradox: The two twins cannot be treated equally, because one of them accelerates while the other twin stays in some constant state of motion.

This example can also be used to illustrate what has been described as a sudden change of speed in section 3.2.4.1. The clock *C1* perfectly fits the definition of a tangential system for the sudden change taking place when *C2* is transferred to *C3*. For the left edge of the combined system *C2-C3* the change takes place at event *M*, for the right edge the change takes place at event *M'*. From the setup of the scenario it follows that the relativistic length relations hold for all (equally built) clocks. Exactly in this case the events *M* and *M'* are simultaneous for C1. At least in this linearized version of an accelerated system it is thus clear that simultaneous change and relativistic lengths relations go hand in hand.

3.3.2 Standard Versus Lorentz-Type Interpretations

Somewhere on the edge of what is taken as serious science, there is still a debate concerned with the interpretation of relativity theory. Leaving aside the camp who claims that relativity theory as a whole is wrong, there is an absolutely arguable set of viewpoints which I summarized as Lorentz-type interpretations[59] of special relativity. Before I go into the alternative Euclidean interpretation, I will briefly summarize the ideas standing behind both established interpretations.

3.3.2.1 The Standard Interpretation

The standard interpretation of special relativity concentrates on Minkowski's geometrical picture,[60] in which a unified *spacetime* plays a kind of ontological role. The line element s^2 of the spacetime geometry integrates space and time distances in the following way:

$$s^2 = x^2 + y^2 + z^2 - c^2 t^2 \qquad (3.19)$$

The line element represents a property of a spacetime distance that remains constant under changes of perspective, i.e. under Lorentz transformations. For so-called time-like spacetime distances, the line element takes a negative value, for space-like distances the line element is positive, and for light the distance vanishes.

Minkowski offers the following reformulation of the line element using the imaginary unit *i*.

---

[59] These interpretations are related to (Lorentz, 1909).
[60] (Minkowski, 1915)

$$s^2 = x^2 + y^2 + z^2 + ic^2t^2 \qquad (3.20)$$
$$i = \sqrt{-1}$$

By this move, Lorentz transformations become pseudo-Euclidean rotations, which on the one hand makes the mathematical treatment easier, and on the other hand provokes speculations about the status of the imaginary time axis.[61]

Minkowski's geometrical formulation not only influenced the interpretation of special relativity, but also paved the way for Einstein's general relativity, which is a generalization to curved spacetime.

The following listing of the main characteristics of the standard interpretation of special relativity makes use of the geometrical formulation.

The spacetime geometry itself has a high, ontological status in the standard interpretation. A spacetime distance between two events is the same for every observer, only the combination of space and time components changes. In addition to the (inside) inertial observers there is no outside observer constructed. Quite to the contrary, any idea of a priviledged point of view is heavily refused. One argument for this is simply the application of Occam's razor: If it is possible to model measured space and time distances without referring to a priviledged frame, then let's get rid of it. There is, however, a deeper reason which is connected to the understanding of time.

A priviledged frame of reference would define an absolute coordinate system including an objective sense of simultaneity. Simultaneity, however, is relative in special relativity. Any two space-like events cannot be objectively ordered in time. The existence of absolute simultaneity is incompatible with the relativity principle, at least in connection with physical effects. From a pre-relativistic understanding of time, though, there must be something like absolute simultaneity as the basis for an objective flow of time.

Consistent with the above said, the speed of causal effects is limited to the speed of light. By this, the time-ordering of cause and effect is preserved under any Lorentz transformation. The limit case, namely signals moving at the speed of light, deserves a closer look. For such a signal, no time at all passes between two events (e.g. emission and absorption). The respective spacetime distance according to the Minkowski geometry is zero for any observer.

The invariance of the vacuum speed of light for any inertial observer is a property of spacetime as such and is not due to any effects concerning the measuring instruments. Length contraction and time dilation are merely *perspective* – relative motion does not make a *real* difference between objects.

---

[61] E.g. (Atmanspacher, 1993).

In the historical context of the creation of relativity theory the concept of an ether played a crucial role. In the traditional understanding any wave needs a medium – the medium for light was a supposed world ether filling all "empty" space. Attempts to experimentally verify the existence of the ether failed, and the special theory of relativity is usually seen as a proof of the non-existence of the ether.

3.3.2.2 Lorentz-type Interpretations

For defenders of a Lorentzian view,[62] there is a twofold ontology concerning space and time. There exists an absolute frame, from whose perspective the substantial medium called *ether* is at rest, and an absolute flow of time. The invariance of the speed of light is valid only for the ether's rest frame and merely apparent for moving frames. Length contraction and time dilation, which depend on motion relative to the ether, are *real* phenomena with respect to the rest frame. The reciprocity of these effects, i.e. the fact that for the really contracted observer the resting observer also appears to be contracted, is due to the real contraction of the moving meter stick and to asynchronous measurements (according to Einstein's definition) performed by the moving observer.

Although I am far away from proposing an interpretation in the spirit of Lorentz, I would like to point out the consistency of the approach. However, I see serious problems mainly in the context of a possible inclusion of gravitation and in the light of a broader understanding of space and time.

As both the standard and Lorentz-type interpretations make the same experimental predictions, the choice between them can only be based upon considerations external to the domain of special relativity. The main argument for adopting the standard interpretation is the fact that the assumption of an absolute rest frame is unnecessary for the development of the theory. Lorentz-type interpretations claim that they allow a classical understanding of special relativity by saving the medium for electromagnetic waves and the intuitive concept of an independent time dimension.

3.3.2.3 The Euclidean Interpretation

The first argument for an alternative interpretation has already been given by the analysis of the normalization problem. Although the above presented two interpretations are significantly different, they can be attacked for the same weakness, namely for the secondary treatment of the normalization problem and consequently for ignoring the role of acceleration for special relativity. I have argued that a clear treatment of the normalization problem makes it necessary to deal with acceleration. Otherwise the normalization of measuring instruments already presupposes the relativity principle and reduces to a mere convention leaving no empirical content for the Lorentz

---

[62] E.g. (Lorentz, 1909; Ehrlichson, 1973; Bell, 1994).

transformations. If, however, special relativity is built upon an assumption on acceleration, a different kind of interpretation of special relativity becomes possible.

3.3.2.3.1 The Outside Geometry

I call this new approach the Euclidean interpretation of special relativity for the simple reason that from the constructed outside view the results of all space and time measurements performed by all observers can be understood on the basis of a completely Euclidean geometry, whose line element is given by:

$$s^2 = x^2 + y^2 + z^2 + c^2 t^2 \qquad (3.21)$$

Unlike in the Minkowski geometry, the line element does not represent a property of a spacetime distance that is constant for all inertial observers. This reflects the fact that in the Euclidean interpretation there is a change occurring when an object or a set of measuring instruments accelerates (which is the precondition for switching to a different frame of reference). However, there is a geometrical property which is conserved under such changes, namely the spacetime volume.

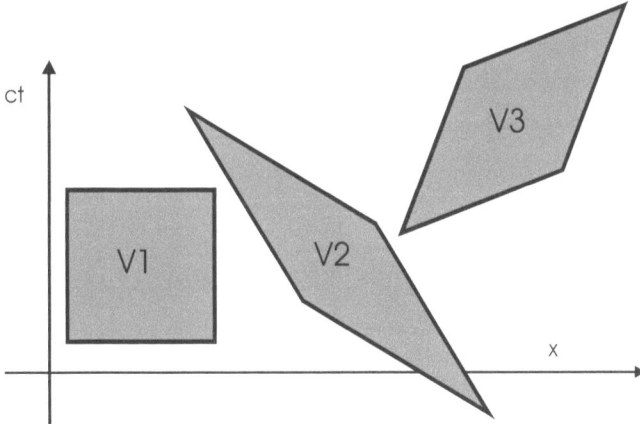

Fig. 3.9. Spacetime cells representing the "same" light clock in different states of constant motion have the same spacetime volume (V1 = V2 = V3).

Fig. 3.9 shows the spacetime cells representing what can be treated as the same observer in different constant states of motion. Their volumes, which are defined in the Euclidean spacetime geometry, are the same. This property is hard to define in the Minkowski geometry, but gives an intuitive understanding of what happens when an object accelerates in the Euclidean interpretation.

3.3.2.3.2 *How to Derive the Lorentz Transformations*

The interpretation of a theory is closely linked to its derivation. According to the suggested interpretation, the Lorentz transformations should be (and have been) developed in a Euclidean spacetime geometry by the following steps:

- *Definition of the measurement procedures according to Einstein.*
- *The assumption that the vacuum speed of light is invariant for one frame, independent of the speed of the source.*
- *The assumption that (ideal) objects accelerate simultaneously from their own point of view (which is equivalent to the assumption that accelerated objects show the Lorentz contraction).*

In this derivation, the relativity principle is missing. However, as a consequence of the Lorentz transformations the relativity principle gets a much stronger status. Unlike in the standard derivation, where the relativity principle boils down to a mere convention for the normalization of measuring instruments, it receives an empirical value in the alternative interpretation.

3.3.2.3.3 *Simultaneous Change Revisited*

As has already been pointed out in section 3.2.4.3, the assumption of simultaneous change requires non-classical properties of matter. Therefore, quantum mechanics could become the basis for special relativity.

For defenders of a Lorentzian view the possibility of simultaneous effects may seem attractive, as it might turn out that quantum mechanical effects are absolutely simultaneous, which would mark the rest frame of the ether.[63] This idea, however, is not supported by the proposed interpretation. The suggested simultaneity of acceleration depends on the motion state of the accelerating object and is not at all absolute. If acceleration was synchronized according to some absolute simultaneity, the Lorentz contraction for accelerated objects would not hold.

From the viewpoint of spacetime holism, the assumption of simultaneous change reflects what has been called the *wave aspect* in the introduction to spacetime holism. The accelerating object maintains its internal relations in space. It does so by coordinating the changes of its parts according to a self-produced simultaneity. By this, the object manifests itself as a self-organizing system. It is even possible to formulate the object's behavior in the language of radical constructivism. Maturana and Varela (1987) define an *autopoietic unit* as a recursive system that is capable of maintaining its internal relations and therefore its operation, when undergoing (non-destructive) changes.

---

[63] K. Popper (1982) suggested to analyze the synchrony of quantum-mechanical effects as a possible test between standard and Lorentz interpretations of special relativity.

If a system, through its operation, brings forth its own, internal time, and if changes in the system take place simultaneously with respect to this internal time, then it is possible that these changes are not perceivable for the (operating) system and thus leave the system unchanged from its own perspective. The internal relations conserved in a referential frame under a change of motion are, e.g. the relation between the length of the meter stick and all other resting lengths within the frame. Through Einstein's definition of the measurement processes, lengths as well as time intervals are operational (inside) conceptions. In good analogy with autopoiesis, lengths and time intervals in their operational meaning are defined recursively, i.e. with regard to each other. What is conserved under a simultaneous change are the relations between these operational concepts.

Following this line of argumentation, it may be suggested that a useful concept of a system should account for the fact that there is a set of relations that remain unchanged from within. Only when this is the case, the system may appear as an entity to the inside observer.

The previous considerations allow to make a distinction between systems and non-systems in special relativity. For the case of the acceleration of physical bodies a prominent example can be used to illustrate this difference.

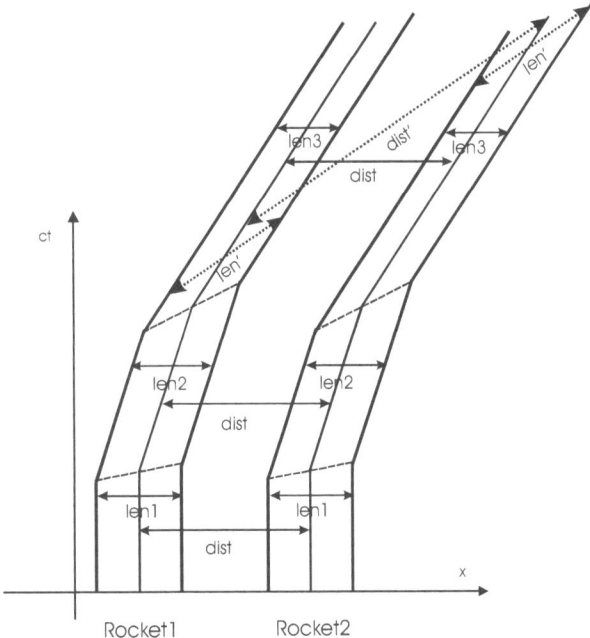

Fig. 3.10. Two rockets are accelerated simultaneously from the view of the resting frame. Their lengths contract, but their distance stays the same. From the view of one of the rockets, the lengths stay identical and the distance between the rockets increases.

Fig. 3.10 shows two rockets that initially rest in the frame of the diagram and undergo two sudden accelerations. These accelerations are equally strong for both rockets and take place at the same time from the view of the rest frame. By this, the principle of simultaneous change is violated for the two rockets taken together and consequently they do not form a system. From the perspective of one of the rockets the distance to the other rocket does not stay the same through the acceleration phases, while its own length is conserved. Thus, each rocket alone can be treated as a system.

3.3.2.3.4 Inside Versus Outside Views

Both the standard interpretation and Lorentz-type interpretations make ontological claims. Spacetime holism, which is very cautious about ontology, rather deals with the distinction between inside and outside concepts of observation. The Euclidean interpretation of relativity theory shows how inside and outside views fit together in a way that makes clear how the outside view is *constructed* from the inside view and how the inside view can be *explained* from the outside view.

The outside view that is suggested as a basis for the alternative interpretation of special relativity is a 4-dimensional and fully Euclidean geometry. The diagrams presented in this chapter are to be understood as 2-dimensional projections of this geometry. The outside view is comparable to the reader's view of the given illustrations. The reader may rotate the sheets of paper and check the diagrams from different perspectives. This, of course, does not relate to a physical process, because the outside observer is not part of what is being illustrated and does not undergo any changes (e.g. the reader's ruler stays the same).

Inside observers cannot be regarded as detached or unaffected when they change their spacetime angle of observation, as their meter sticks and clocks do not stay the same. It is the inside observer transformation that is described by the Lorentz transformations. The Minkowski spacetime geometry, which captures measurements stemming from inside observers, can *in principle* not take an ontological status in the above defined sense.

Claiming that the geometry of space and time *is* a Minkowski geometry may very easily be understood as an outside observer's statement, though. A good example for this is given by Stephen Hawking's cosmology.[64] He illustrates his view of the universe by the use of a diagram of a spacetime sphere defined in a Minkowski-type geometry, i.e. with an imaginary time axis. From the Euclidean perspective, there is a deep conceptual mistake standing behind this picture, which boils down to a mixture of what usually is called *inter-subjectivity* and *objectivity*. For sure, objective knowledge as such cannot be achieved, but as a useful cognitive tool it is must be clearly separated from inter-subjective knowledge. The subjects of relativity theory are the reference frames holding

---

[64] (Hawking, 1988).

their operational concepts of space and time. The Minkowski spacetime geometry including the Lorentz transformation describes nothing else but their inter-subjective agreement on space and time measurements. Objective knowledge is a quite different type of knowledge based on the idea of a non-involved, non-operating observer who is not subject to changes and who sees things *as they are*.

The 4-dimensional Euclidean world of the alternative interpretation also contrasts the twofold ontology of Lorentz-type interpretations consisting of a 3-dimensional space and a 1-dimensional time. These interpretations concentrate on an outside view of space and time. A good example of its secondary treatment of inside observation is the question whether light *really* has a constant speed or just *appears* to be constant to all observers. As a defender of the primacy of the inside, operational view one could easily reply that the speed of light is constant in the sense that speed has to be defined in operational terms – being measured to the same value thus means to be the same.

From the constructed outside view of the Euclidean interpretation there is one frame whose space and time axes appear as orthogonal lines, yet this frame should not be regarded as the absolute rest frame as is done by Lorentz-type interpretations. Notions like space, time, motion or rest are – in the last consequence - meaningless for the outside observer and have to be understood as mere inside observer categories. The outside picture is completely static and leaves no room for an independent, dynamical time dimension.

From the alternative perspective, the key for a deeper understanding of relativity has to be sought in the nature of the physical object and its relation to the 4-dimensional whole. The existence of the physical object (i.e. system) is bound to two types of connections. On the one hand the object maintains itself through time, on the other hand, as has been suggested, the spatially separate parts of the object must be coordinated simultaneously through space. The alternative interpretation - aiming at the construction of a consistent *outside* view - requires the analysis of these – from the *inside* - very different connections on a common ground. This common ground is provided by spacetime holism.

In some sense the Euclidean interpretation is more radical than both established interpretations. More explicitly than in the Lorentz interpretation, the understanding of special relativity is based on a constructed outside view. From this outside view, however, the integration of space and time into an inseparable whole reaches even further than in the standard interpretation, where space and time still receive a different treatment.

3.3.2.3.5 *What Makes Space and Time Different?*

For the outside Euclidean geometry there does not exist any difference between space and time dimensions; in other words, the dimension which is experienced as time by inside observers is nothing but another space dimension for the outside observer. But how can the experienced difference between space and time be explained from the outside view? An answer to this question becomes possible, once the universe is understood as a 4-dimensional "object" with certain structural properties, as is suggested by spacetime holism.

As an illustration of this, consider the following example: If the trunk of a tree is described in 3-dimensional space, an observer can recognize structural differences in different directions, e.g. the fibrous structure of the wood. However, nobody would say that this structure, which might be oriented along the observer's z-axis, is a property of the z-axis. If the tree is cut down, or if the observer looks from a different angle, the wood's structure would no longer be a z-structure (for an "inside" woodworm the situation would, of course, be different). In a similar way the obvious differences between space and time are not due to a special role of one of the outside observer's dimensions, but have to be regarded as properties of the 4-dimensional "object" called universe (better: of some region of the universe).

For a theory of time, the starting point must be to understand objects as well as inside observers themselves as sub-structures of the 4-dimensional whole. What appears as a temporal relation to an inside observer has to be understood as a spacetime relation with some specific structural properties, just as spacetime relations with some other properties would be interpreted as spatial relations by the inside observer.

In chapter 7 I will discuss spacetime holism's approach to time, which is built upon the presented understanding of spacetime.

As a last remark in this section, I would like to connect the understanding of the universe as a 4-dimensional object to the assumption of an ether. Indeed, there is no empty space for the Euclidean interpretation, but unlike for Lorentz-type interpretations, the ether has to be conceived of as 4-dimensional. The problems with the traditional concept stem from treating the objects and the ether as separate things. Only in this case there should be some relative movement, which cannot be measured, though. In spacetime holism, the object is treated as a sort of contraction of the "spacetime stuff," which is much in accord with what general relativity says about the relation between a gravitational object and the spacetime geometry.

3.4 Towards a Euclidean General Relativity[65]

In geometrical terms, the Euclidean interpretation of special relativity is made possible by embedding the inside Minkowski geometry of the standard interpretation into an outside Euclidean geometry. It is only consequent to investigate a possible extension of this idea to general relativity: Can general relativity be embedded into an outside Euclidean geometry? When thinking of singularities in the curved geometry of general relativity (e.g. black holes), there is not much hope for a positive answer.

In this section, I will introduce an intuitive beginning for what might become a new *Euclidean general relativity*, which is based on a Euclidean outside view also for general relativity. Other than the presented Euclidean approach to special relativity, which is just a different interpretation leaving all the formulas and experimental predictions unchanged, the suggested Euclidean general relativity is a different theory making different predictions, at least for strong gravitational fields (e.g. no black holes and no time loops).

3.4.1 The Basic Assumptions of the Euclidean General Relativity

The following three assumptions lay the basis for the suggested approach to general relativity.

(1) Special relativity is the limiting case of general relativity.

(2) Free fall is inertial motion.

(3) From an outside view, the speed of light in a gravitational field depends on the distance to a gravitational object (i.e. on gravitational potential) and on direction. Incoming light is faster, while outgoing light is slower.[66]

The assumptions (1) and (2) are adopted from standard general relativity, assumption (3) makes sense only for a hypothetical outside observer who is not affected by gravitation. Therefore, it only seems to be in contradiction to standard general relativity; as a mere outside observer's statement assumption (3) cannot be judged by inside measurements. For inside observers, the speed of light in a gravitational field is always (at least locally) measured to the same value in all directions.

For illustration, I will make use of the concept of a light clock, which has already been introduced in section 3.2.2.1.

---

[65] Some of the ideas in this section have been published in (Winkler, 2002a).
[66] As will be suggested in section 3.4.6, the light speeds in the center of a gravitational field are different.

3.4.2 Outside Rotation and Inside View

A very simple and intuitive example illustrating the possibility of different light speeds in different directions according to assumption (3) is given by an outside spacetime rotation in a Euclidean geometry.

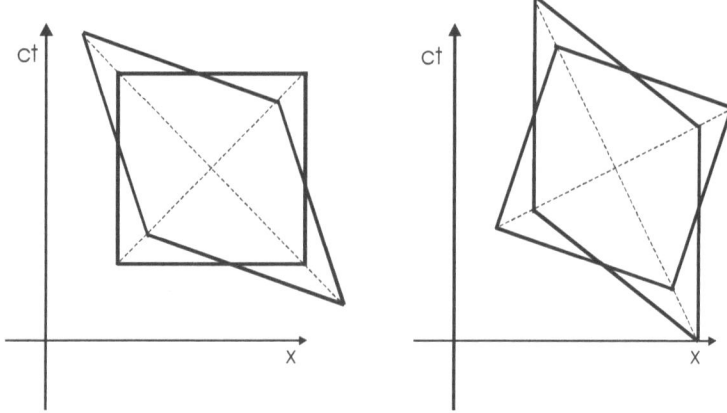

Fig. 3.11. An outside rotation of the spacetime units belonging to inertial observers in relative motion. From the outside, the speed of light in the rotated scenario differs from c and depends on direction. From the inside, i.e. for the involved inertial observer, there is no difference between the rotated and the non-rotated scenario.

Fig. 3.11 shows two scenarios involving the spacetime units of inertial observers in relative motion. The second scenario is rotated from an outside view, which implies that the speed of light differs from c and depends on direction. However, this difference is visible only from the outside; from the inside, the speed of light is constant for all observers and there is no difference between the two scenarios. Therefore, special relativity is valid also in the rotated case.

This idea can be generalized to all possible combinations of different light speeds. Locally, the speed of light will always be the same in all directions, as long as simultaneity is defined (according to Einstein) on the basis of light. As an extension of the idea behind Fig. 3.9, I assume that a light clock, which is brought to a different spacetime location with different light speeds, will still have the same spacetime volume. This gives us a basis for comparing the scales of distant light clocks from an outside view: Two observers use the *same* scales of space and time (meters and seconds), if the volumes of their spacetime units are identical.

3.4.3 Light Clocks in a Gravitational Field

The intuitive idea that the speeds of light in a gravitational field can be understood as "rotated" from an outside perspective allows an explanation of gravitational time dilation.

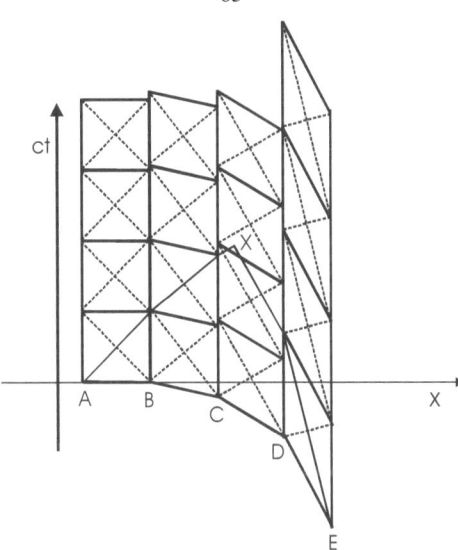

Fig. 3.12. Resting light clocks in a gravitational field from an outside view. The speed of light depends on the distance to the center of gravity (somewhere on the right side) and on direction: outgoing light beams are slower, incoming light beams are faster than light beams far away from the gravitational object. Light clocks that are closer to the gravitational object go slower. The events A and E are not simultaneous, as the meeting point X of light beams started at A and E is not located in the middle.

Fig. 3.12 shows four light clocks resting in a gravitational field whose center lies somewhere on the right side of the diagram. The differences in the speed of light according to assumption (3) result in spacetime units that are not only "stretched" as is the case for moving clocks in special relativity (see Fig. 3.9), but also rotated according to Fig. 3.11. Note that the continuous changes of the light velocities are simplified to discrete changes in order to show the connection to special relativity. In the infinitesimal limit, the light clocks can locally be treated in the same way as in special relativity, which has been addressed in assumption (1). Comparing the time intervals of the resting light clocks makes clear that time is slower for observers located close to the center of gravity than for observers far away from the center of gravity. By this, gravitational red-shift is explained. It also can be read from the diagram that the simultaneity relation between events looses transitivity. Although A, B, C, D, and E form a chain of locally simultaneous events, the events A and E are not simultaneous; the meeting of light beams started in A and E takes place at event X which is not located in the middle.

3.4.4 Free Fall as Inertial Motion

Fig. 3.13 shows a light clock free falling in a gravitational field. The trajectory of the light clock is a consequence of assumption (2) stating that free fall is inertial motion. From this it follows that the clock has to move such that the reflected light beams always meet in its middle. The differences in the light speeds depending on location force the light clock, which at the beginning moves away from the center of gravity, to change direction and to finally move toward the center of gravity.

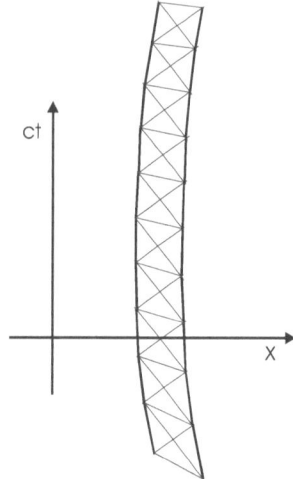

Fig. 3.13. A free falling light clock in a gravitational field. Obeying the law of inertial motion, the light clock that initially moves away from the gravitational object changes direction and accelerates towards the gravitating object.

3.4.5 Free Fall and Volume Conservation

It seems very difficult to put the law of inertial motion, which has been the basis of Fig. 3.13, into mathematical form. However, the following suggestion could not only help solving this problem, but has also nice consequences for a deeper intuitive understanding.

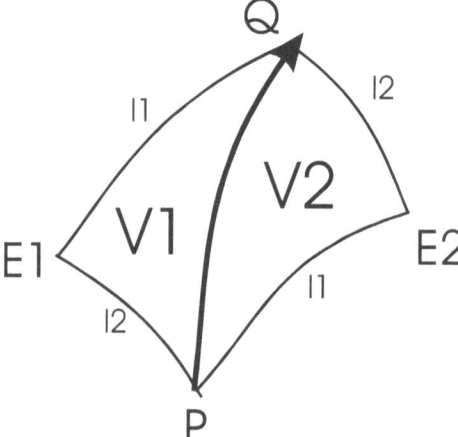

Fig. 3.14. A trajectory piece PQ of a test particle in a gravitational field. The simultaneous emission, reflection, and simultaneous absorption of light beams in both direction produces the spacetime volumes V1 and V2.

Fig. 3.14 shows a trajectory piece PQ of a free falling test particle in a gravitational field. On the basis of the local light trajectories $l1$ and $l2$ two spacetime areas $V1$ and $V2$ are constructed. The hypothetical reflection events $E1$ and $E2$ are chosen such that light beams emitted in P meet again Q. Note that the two curves both named $l1$ are in general not parallel, the same holds for $l2$.

By the use of Fig. 3.14 the assumption on free fall can be formulated.

For small pieces of the trajectory of a free falling test particle, the spacetime volumes $V1$ and $V2$ are identical.

Given the light speeds and their changes in the investigated spacetime region, and given the speed of a test particle in some starting event, the trajectory should be fully defined by this assumption on equal volumes. If it is possible to formulate a motion law out of these considerations, this motion law would automatically be co-variant, i.e. it would be valid for all possible observers. Why is this so?

The fact that different observers, respectively their spacetime units, can be mapped to each other by a transformation that conserves their volume has a simple consequence: If two spacetime volumes (or areas) are the same for one observer, then they are the same for all observers. A law that is formulated exclusively in terms of volumes (or areas) is therefore form invariant to observer transformations.

Due to the lack of mathematical expertise, my attempts to find a mathematical formulation of the suggested motion law did not produce much more than the following intuitive idea, which, however, shows how Newtonian free fall appears as an approximation.

Small pieces of the trajectory of a free falling object can be treated as if they had a constant speed. The same holds for pieces of the local light trajectories. Let us regard the local speed of the object as a combination of the two light speeds.

$$v(object) = A \cdot v(l1) + B \cdot v(l2) \qquad (3.22)$$
$$A + B = 1$$

The change of the speed of the object is supposed to be a combination of the changes of the light speeds.

$$\Delta v(object) = A \cdot \Delta v(l1) + B \cdot \Delta v(l2) \qquad (3.23)$$

This formula, which is an attempt to capture the idea of spacetime volume conservation, describes only a discrete step of what is a continuous evolution: All the variables undergo continuous changes; $l1$ and $l2$ depend on the location of the object, which changes according to the object's speed, and also the values of A and B vary.

In Newtonian gravitation, all objects (and even light) at the same location fall with the same acceleration, independent on the speed of the object. This is not the case in the suggested approach. However, for small speeds (where A and B are close to equal), all objects can be said to show the same acceleration. Light, though, falls differently, as will be suggested in the following section.

3.4.6 Light Trajectories in the Gravitational Field

In Euclidean general relativity, everything depends on the light trajectories in a given region of spacetime. If the light trajectories in a gravitational field look like suggested in Fig. 3.15, there is an acceleration towards the center of gravity in each location guaranteed for all objects whose speed is far below that of light.

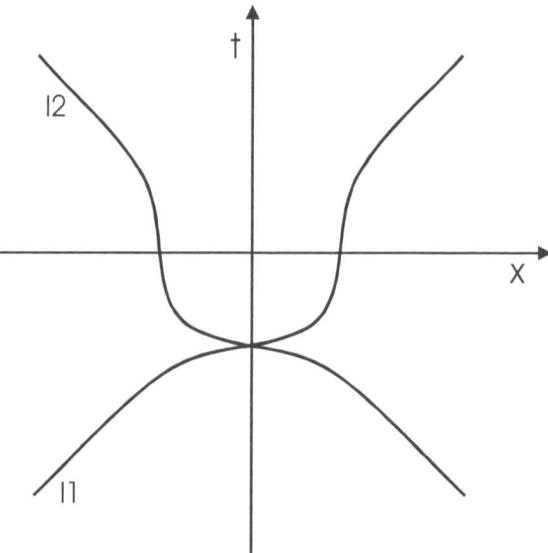

Fig. 3.15. The suggested light trajectories in a gravitational field.

In addition, the suggested light trajectories allow to understand the object, as it is treated in special relativity, as an approximation of the gravitational field.

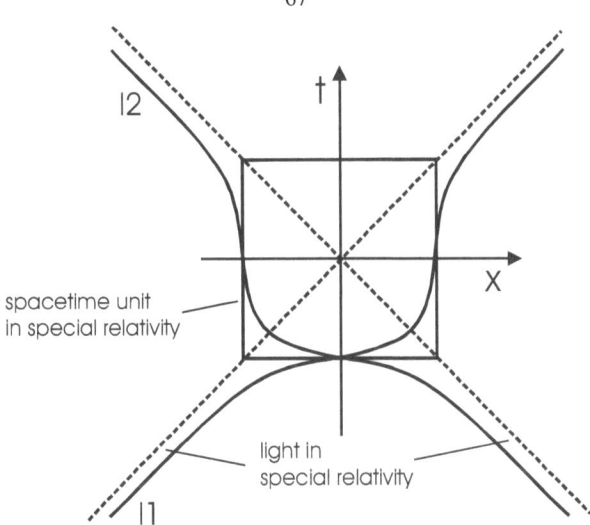

Fig. 3.16. The object in special relativity, which is represented by a spacetime unit, can be seen as an approximation of the gravitational field in the Euclidean general relativity.

Fig. 3.16 shows how the spacetime unit of an object in special relativity fits into the supposed light trajectories of the Euclidean general relativity. For moving gravitational fields, the light trajectories can be derived from the resting case by a Lorentz transformation of the diagram (Fig. 3.17).

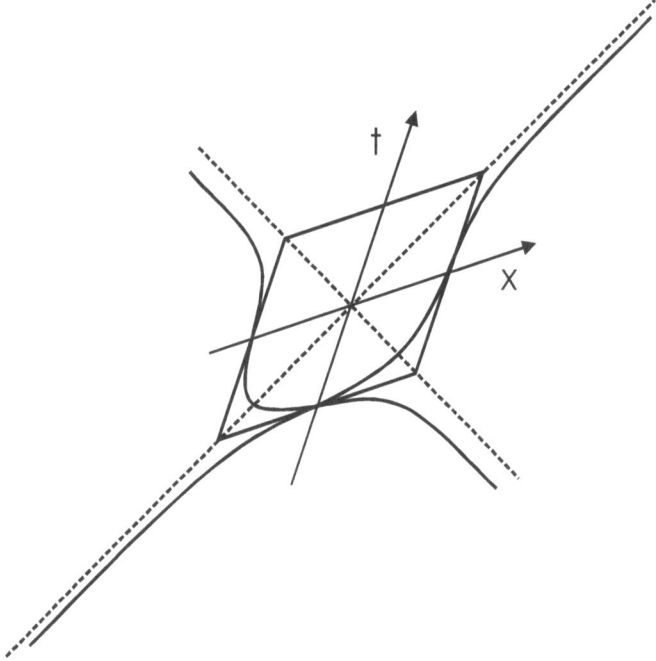

Fig. 3.17. The scenario of the previous illustration after a Lorentz transformation.

3.4.7 Continuity and Discontinuity in the Gravitational Field

As a consequence of the light trajectories in the gravitational field, the spacetime units of objects resting in different locations can be drawn.

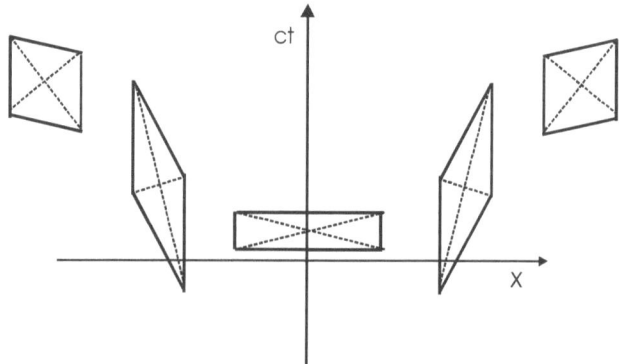

Fig. 3.18. Spacetime units of objects resting at different locations in a gravitational field.

Fig. 3.18 shows different spacetime units,[67] the first and fifth far away from the center of gravity, the second and forth rather close to the center, and the third one in the center. While the first type still resembles the spacetime unit in special relativity, the second type shows increased temporal continuity (gravitational time dilation) and strong spatial discontinuity. In the center of the gravitational field, the situation is reversed; there is less temporal continuity and less spatial discontinuity. This picture shows exactly what has been introduced as external particle and internal wave aspects of systems in section 2.3. Gravitation can thus can be seen as a separator of spatial and temporal structure.

3.4.8 Discussion

While I consider the arguments for the Euclidean view of special relativity to be hard enough to be taken serious by theoretical physicists, the suggested Euclidean perspective for a new general relativity is far from being elaborated; it might be regarded as a "mere speculation." However, I think that the context of spacetime holism provides a sufficient basis for pursuing the approach. On the one hand spacetime holism requires an alternative approach to general relativity for reasons of consistency with the Euclidean interpretation of special relativity; on the other hand spacetime holism's account of time (see chapter 7) is incompatible with black holes and time loops, which are very well allowed by Einstein's general relativity, but do not have any basis in the Euclidean general relativity.

Though not being formalized, the Euclidean general relativity can give at least qualitative explanations of the experimentally confirmed statements of general relativity, namely light bending and gravitational time dilation. In addition to that, there is an experimental prediction following from Euclidean general relativity that clearly deviates from the standard theory: As can be read from Fig. 3.18, time goes faster for observers resting in the center of a gravitational field. Therefore, the frequency of e.g. electromagnetic waves emitted from the center of a gravitational object should be higher compared to the frequency of the same waves when being emitted far away from the center; in standard general relativity these waves are supposed to show a lower frequency.

3.5 Summary

It has been shown in this chapter that spacetime holism and relativity theory can be fruitfully related to each other. The Euclidean interpretation, which is a much more intuitive way of understanding relativity theory, has been developed on the basis of spacetime holism's distinction between inside and outside views and systems theoretical properties, which are compatible with spacetime holism, as well. The suggested treatment of general relativity results in an even stronger link to spacetime

---

[67] The diagram which shows equal volumes of the spacetime units in the x-t plane is not fully correct – it is the 4-dimensional volume that should be the same.

holism by providing a possible basis for the structural notions of spatial and temporal continuity and discontinuity in the spacetime continuum.

4 Information Processing

Contribution to the Thesis
The paradigm of information processing which still dominates in cognitive science is criticized for its separate treatment of space and time structures. It is shown, though, that the case for an integrated view of space and time can be made in the domain of information processing itself. The example of chess programming reveals that meaning and computation show the duality relation which is postulated by spacetime holism.

4.1 Introduction

In the history of Artificial Intelligence and Cognitive Science[68] the paradigm of information processing played a unifying role for a couple of decades. Despite a lot of fundamental critique,[69] the idea to understand and study human intelligence as the processing of information still rules.

The central idea standing behind the paradigm of information processing is the assumption that thought processes can be formalized.[70] Formalization means that the semantics of a given problem, though not captured as such in the formal representation, is conserved under mere syntactical (computational) transformations ("Take care of the syntax, the semantics will follow.").

Quite in line with this, and as will be discussed in section 5.2, the traditional program of artificial intelligence is based on the assumption that cognition can be understood as the (mere syntactical) computation of meaningful symbols.

Before criticizing this view of cognition and suggesting an alternative in chapter 5, I will show how two main assumptions of spacetime holism, namely the inseparability of space and time, and the first fundamental duality relation between space and time structure, can be given meaning in the context of information processing.

4.2 The Unity of Information and Processing

From the viewpoint of spacetime holism, the separation of information and processing, which stands behind the information processing paradigm, very much resembles the traditional separation between space and time. On the one hand there are information, data and representations that can be treated as spatial entities, on the other hand there are processes and algorithms that can be treated as temporal entities.

---

[68] E.g. (Gardner, 1988).
[69] See chapter 5.3.
[70] In most but not all cases what can be formalized can be computed.

It is clear to every computer programmer that both domains are highly interrelated, but the principled conclusion is usually avoided. Arguing for an inseparable unity of information and processing, however, is easy and can be done within the domain of computation itself.

There is not just one way for a programmer to model a problem of information processing. Different views of *one-and-the-same* problem result in models with different amounts of information and processing. We should not ask: "How much information (or processing) is required to solve the task?", but "How much information-processing do we need?".

As an example, think of the task of storing images. We can store pixels with a high cost of information space and little cost of processing. Or we can store graphical objects (like circles or rectangles) that have to be extracted from and re-transformed into pixels. The amount of processing will be higher and the amount of information will be lower. There is no right information and no right processing in a similar way as there is no right spatial and no right temporal extension of a physical process.

The suggested unity of information and processing can be seen as the cause of tremendous practical problems in software engineering, where for a long time data and process models were treated as more or less separable issues. Especially when software projects are big and when changing requirements demand a constant re-design, enormous costs are produced by the fact that changes in the data model very often have highly non-local effects on the algorithms and therefore for the processes. The reverse is also true: Changes in the required functionality have a high and costly impact on the representation of the data.

Though the problem is fundamental, there is a better way to deal with it. In the so-called *object-oriented paradigm* of software engineering, information and processing come closer to each other. The *object,* which comprises data and algorithms, and which ought to be an intuitively meaningful unit to the human programmer (and sometimes also to the user), allows to keep most changes local.

Another argument for the inseparability of information and processing follows from the fact that information as such, without being processed, is a completely meaningless term. To use a phrase of Gregory Bateson (1972), "information is a difference that makes a difference." Without something or somebody knowing what to do with the "difference," there is no information. Even the mere quantitative account of information in Shannon's model[71] presupposes the computation of probabilities.

---

[71] (Shannon, 1948)

4.3 The Duality Between Meaning and Computation

Spacetime holism's first fundamental duality relation leads to what has been named wave and particle aspects. Computation, which already appeared in the disguise of Laplace's demon, stands for the particle aspect composed of continuity in time and discontinuity in space. In the context of information processing, the wave aspect can be identified with the term meaning denoting relations in the space of data or representations.

The following section, which is the outcome of a collaboration with Johannes Fürnkranz (Winkler & Fürnkranz, 1998), shows the duality relation between meaning and computation using the example of chess programs. The aspect of meaning appears as the term *human-compatible knowledge*, while the aspect of computation appears as the term *machine-compatible processing*. The discussion includes reflections on the state and possible orientation of artificial intelligence as a consequence of the duality relation.

4.4 A Hypothesis on the Divergence of AI Research

Artificial Intelligence has been conceived as the science of both programming computers to perform intelligent tasks and devising computational models of human reasoning. Originally, both aspects were considered to go hand in hand, but it soon became apparent that AI research is determined to split into a cognitive branch and an engineering branch which correspond to these two objectives respectively. Research in computer chess is a prominent and most successful example for this development. We conjecture that the reason for this divergence is a non-linear interaction between associative human knowledge structures on the one hand and the strict algorithmic processing requirements of computational models on the other hand.

In its early days, Artificial Intelligence (AI) had the two-fold goal of, on the one hand, providing computers with the ability of solving tasks that are commonly perceived as requiring intelligence, and, on the other hand, furthering our understanding of human thinking.

"If one could devise a successful chess machine, one would seem to have penetrated to the core of human intellectual endeavour." (Newell, Shaw & Simon, 1958)

The above quotation by Newell, Shaw and Simon exemplifies this view: On the one hand we want to achieve intelligent functionality (". . . devise a successful chess machine . . . "), while, on the other hand, we aim at understanding the processes that guide human reasoning (". . . penetrating to the core of human intellectual endeavour.").

Furthermore, it was believed that both aspects of AI go hand in hand: A better understanding of the human intellect is facilitated by the ability to test computational models of cognitive theories, and, conversely, the achievement of intelligent functionality is impossible without a deeper study of how we human beings achieve that functionality. Hence, Newell, Shaw and Simon were convinced that a successful construction of a computer that excels in chess, commonly perceived as a task whose mastery requires intelligence, would have a strong impact on Artificial Intelligence in general.

Now, that the Deep Blue team has devised a successful chess machine, it is apparent that, although significant progress has been made in both, our understanding of human cognition and the implementation of intelligent machines, we are not much closer to the original goal of AI, of implementing a genuine artificial intelligence on a computer. Instead, research in AI has diverged into two independent research areas: On the one hand, the what one might call cognitive branch of AI (nowadays usually referred to as Cognitive Science) puts a strong emphasis on the psychological validity of computational models, in particular with respect to knowledge representation and memory organization. On the other hand, we have the engineering branch of AI, which is motivated by solving particular tasks, and is mostly concerned with finding formalizations and software architectures that are tailored to the solution of a specific problem and can be efficiently executed on computer hardware. Deep Blue is a most prominent example for this line of research.

In the following, we illustrate this split of AI into two different branches by classifying research in the domain of chess along two different axes: human-compatible knowledge (HCK) and machine-compatible processing (MCP). We further argue on the example domain of chess that the successes of AI research can be found along the two axes, but have not yet penetrated into the white area which we consider to contain the core problems of AI. We then ask the question why this is the case, and present a hypothesis to resolve this issue.

4.4.1 Two Illustrative Examples

The basic problem that AI has to face for achieving its original goal of finding computational models of human cognition is to integrate the abstract concepts that human beings usually use for problem solving with the strict algorithmic processing definitions that are required for implementing programs on a computer. To illustrate these dimensions consider the two problems depicted in Fig. 4.1.

Nenad Petrović, 1969 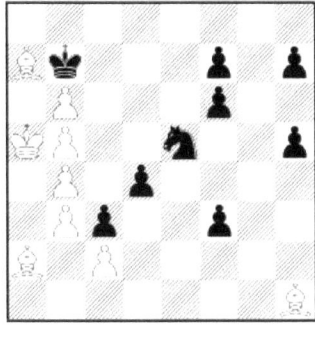 Sam Loyd, 1892

Mate in 270 moves　　　　　　Mate in 2 moves

Fig. 4.1 A knowledge-rich and a knowledge-poor problem.

The first problem is a slightly unusual endgame position, but, after some deliberation, a trained chess player will detect many concepts that are familiar from other endgames. For example, it will soon become obvious that black has a dangerous threat with 1. . . d3, which will either queen the d-pawn or distract white's c-pawn, thus allowing black to queen his own c-pawn. Because of the above drawing chance for black, white's only hope lies in queening one of its pawns on the b-file (after playing 1.Bb1 to prevent 1. . . d3). To achieve this, white has to conquer the square a6. However, he has no moves that put black into zugzwang, because black can answer all white king moves with king moves b7-a8-b7. A typical maneuver in such position is the so-called triangle maneuver, where one king is able to use a 3-cycle to return to its original square, while the other king is only able to make a 2-cycle. White can therefore try to move its king to e1, playing e1-f2-f1-e1, which would gain one move. When the white king returns to a5, we will have exactly the same position, but with black to move. As he cannot move his king because of white's threat Ka6, he has to move one of his pawns. Then the entire sequence is repeated 11 times until black has no more pawn moves and has to answer 254. Ka5 with Kc8 thus allowing Ka6, followed by a mate in 15.

Trained chess players could solve this problem in their heads (maybe with the exception of the final mate in 15). However, because of their lack of high-level chess-specific concepts and general problem-solving knowledge, this problem is very hard for current computer chess programs, as the solution is too deep to be found with exhaustive search. A brief experiment that we have conducted with Fritz4 has demonstrated that the program will play Bb1 to prevent black from playing d4-d3, bring its king to a1, Ba2, king to e1, Bb1, and finally move the king to f2 in order to capture the pawn on f3. It does not realize that black then has an easy draw by trading its knight for the bishop and playing f6-f5 thereafter.

Conversely, the second position is quite hard for human chess players, because it does not offer many familiar patterns which could be used for narrowing down the search. The pieces seem to be randomly scattered around the board, thus offering no orientation at all. The only obvious feature is the lack of king safety, so that white should be much better off and probably has a mate in a few moves. However, the restriction to look for a mate in 2 proves to be very hard for a player untrained in solving chess problems, because of the lack of familiar patterns that allow to cut down the number of candidate moves in a reasonable way. She would more or less have to perform an exhaustive search through the numerous possible threats, a procedure for which human memory organization is not particularly well-suited.[72]

On the other hand, positions like these are no different to other positions for a computer chess playing program, and thus it would find the mate as easily as it would find other mate-in-2's, as e.g. the queen sacrifice followed by a smothered mate that every experienced chess player is familiar with. The reason for this is that these algorithms are not modeled after human memory and thus do not have to rely on the recognition of familiar concepts on the board as human chess players do. Instead they rely on state-of-the-art search algorithms that are tailored to be efficiently executable on computer hardware.

We believe that these examples illustrate fairly well the two different aspects of problem solving in which humans and machine respectively excel: On the one hand there is a rich associative memory that is very hard to formalize, while on the other hand there is fast processing of low-level concepts, which is hard to explain in an intuitive way. In the next sections, we will discuss these two aspects in more detail, before we propose a hypothesis on why it is so hard to reconcile them.

4.4.2 Human-compatible knowledge

Chess is probably the game that has been most deeply investigated from a theoretical point of view. Chess books are full of comprehensible knowledge about different aspects of the game. We would like to call such knowledge human-compatible, because it enables a chess student to increase his understanding and competence of the game. Nevertheless, it is mostly unclear how the student uses this knowledge for problem-solving. Human subjects are often able to specify the abstract concepts they use for problem-solving, but are unable to specify the problem-solving process in an exact algorithmic way. For example, a chess player has no problems in explaining the reasoning that made him prefer a certain move over other possible continuations. Analyses like "The move b4

---

[72] Note that a player with experience in solving chess problems would face much less difficulties in solving this problem, because he can rely on appropriate high-level concepts: the queen appears to be underused, so we should look for a mating pattern with the queen (like on e3), and the move Rg3 creates a flight, so this is a good first try. Again, it is important to note that the solution has been discovered by the use of abstract concepts that are hard to formalize, as we will discuss in the following.

gives me a backward pawn on c3, but it prevents a black liberation with a5, so that I can attack his weak a6-pawn on the half-open a-file." are full of abstract concepts like backward pawn, half-open file, etc. that are well-understood by human players. However, it is comparatively difficult for human players to specify the thought processes that made them prefer, e.g., the opponent's weak a6-pawn over their own backward pawn on c3.

Research in chess psychology[73] has extensively analyzed verbal thinking-aloud protocols of chess players of different strengths. The results are that differences in playing strength between experts and novices are not so much due to differences in the ability to calculate long move sequences, but to the use of a library of chess patterns and accompanying moves and plans that helps them choose the right moves for deeper investigations. Several authors have even tried to measure the magnitude of this pattern library, resulting in estimates in the range of 5,000 to 10,000 patterns[74]. Some of these so-called chunks[75] are easy to articulate and common to most chess players (like, e.g., passed pawn, skewer, minority attack), while others are presumably subconscious and subjective to individual players. However, even simple concepts like a knightfork are non-trivial to formalize.[76]

Because of this strong focus on models for memory organization, early AI research has concentrated on the simulation of aspects of the problem-solving process that are closely related to memory, like perception (Simon & Barenfeld, 1969) or retrieval (Simon & Gilmartin, 1973). Recently, these ideas were re-investigated and integrated into the CHREST program (Gobet, 1993), which is the most advanced computational model of a chess player's memory organization. CHUMP is a variant of this program that is actually able to play a game by retrieving moves that it has previously associated to certain chunks in the program's pattern memory (Gobet & Jansen, 1994).

4.4.3 Machine-compatible Processing

AI has soon recognized the difficulty of formalizing human thought in a top-down way (using the human concepts as a starting point), and has instead discovered approaches to solving intelligent tasks which are more closely designed to fit the processing requirements of a computer. Brute-force chess programs are the best-known example of this line of research. The basic idea of brute-force chess programs dates back to (Shannon, 1950) and (Turing, 1953), where one can already find

---

[73] E.g. (deGroot, 1965), (Chase & Simon, 1988), (Holding, 1985), (deGroot, 1996).
[74] (Simon & Chase, 1973), (Hayes, 1987)
[75] Recent research has extended the chunking theory with so-called templates (Gobet & Simon, 1996), i.e., long-term memory structures that are quite similar to scripts and frames, but are based on a detailed psychological model (deGroot & Gobet, 1996). For our discussion, the differences in the details of the psychological models of chunks and templates are irrelevant.
[76] The basic pattern for a fork is a protected knight threatening two higher-valued pieces, like, e.g., rook and queen. However, this simple pattern might not work if the forking knight is pinned. But then again, maybe the knight can give a discovered check.. .

many of the ideas that are still used in today's chess programs (like, e.g., search extensions). However, early chess programs (see (Newell, Shaw & Simon, 1958) for an overview) relied on highly selective search that evaluated positions based on a few basic concepts like material balance, center control, and king safety. This selective search was motivated by both hardware limitations and the attempt to model machine chess playing after human chess playing.

However, the somewhat unexpected success of the Tech program (Gillogly, 1972) for the first time demonstrated the power of brute-force computing. Further improvements on the search algorithms and evaluation functions (Slate & Atkin, 1983) and advances in parallel processing (Hyatt, Gower & Nelson, 1985) and chess-specific hardware[77] have eventually lead to the Deep Blue vs. Kasparov challenge, which resulted in the longawaited defeat of the human world chess champion in a match in 1997, after he had lost the first game under tournament conditions in a previous match in 1996.

4.4.4 Two Dimensions of AI Models

The success of brute-force programs is attributable to the fact that their basic architecture is adapted to what computers are good at: fast calculation using only a few isolated chess concepts, which can be evaluated efficiently. Thus the success of these programs depends on machine-compatible processing (MCP). On the other hand, we have seen that human chess players calculate relatively few moves, but rely on a huge pattern library that helps them select the right move. Thus, their success depends on the availability of human-compatible knowledge (HCK). In the following, we attempt to classify a few AI models in the domain of chess with respect to their contribution along either axis.

A perfect chess program that has access to the perfect game-theoretic values of each position (e.g., by exhaustive search until check-mate) would be on the right end of the MCP axis with no contribution on the HCK axis, as its internal knowledge representation does not contribute in any way to a better understanding of human reasoning. The best-known approximation of this principle is the Deep Blue chess program. The other extreme would be an oracle that could derive the best move in each position from general principles and explain this choice in a clear and understandable form. Chess theory can be viewed as an attempt to approximate this knowledge and Garry Kasparov, in some sense, can be viewed as a machine that embodies this knowledge. Thus he appears high up on the HCK axis, with almost no contribution along the MCP axis.

A project like CHUMP (see above) is strongly motivated by human memory organization, and its processing is not very compatible with typical computer hardware. For example, the program uses artificial simulations of human long-term and short-term memory. Therefore, it has only made a

---

[77] See (Condon & Thompson, 1982), (Ebeling, 1987), (Hsu, 1987).

small step along the MCP axis. Its contribution along the HCK axis is higher, but it is clearly a simplification compared to human memory organization. As a sort of dual example, consider PARADISE (Wilkins, 1980), which is a program for solving chess combinations at an abstract level. The main goal of this project was to investigate the extent to which tree search can be guided and controlled with the use of background knowledge (Wilkins, 1982). The used concepts are quite abstract and clearly motivated by human knowledge, but the processing is still very machine-compatible, using a systematic best-first search in the space of possible plans.

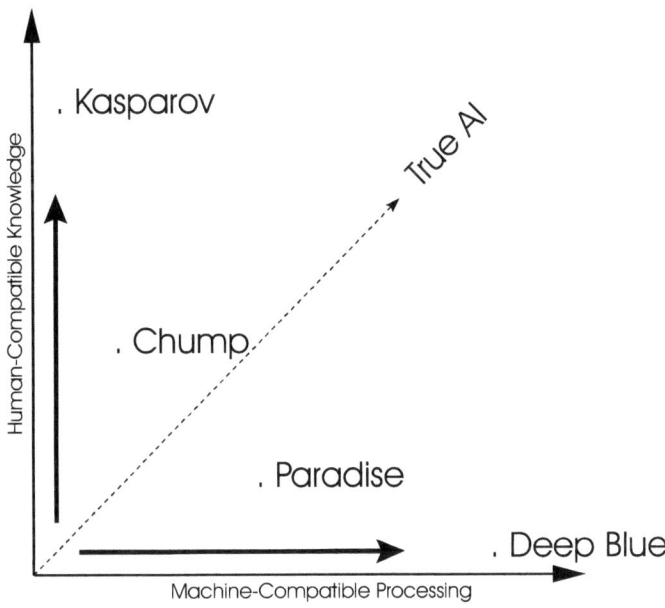

Fig. 4.2 Models of chess playing classified along the two dimensions of human-compatible knowledge (HCK) and machine-compatible processing (MCP).

As we have elaborated above, we view Artificial Intelligence as a science that has to integrate both aspects: human-compatible knowledge and machine-compatible process definitions. Hence, an AI project can be evaluated by its contribution along either axis. Fig. 4.2 positions the "chess models" discussed in the previous paragraphs in this two-dimensional field. We view the overall value of a model as the sum of the contributions that it makes along either axis. Intuitively, for a chess program, this value measures the program's competence in terms of playing strength and explanatory power.

A research program appears as a line progressing through this two-dimensional space. The ideal AI research program should follow the diagonal between the two axes, thus taking into account both aspects equally. The further a research program deviates from this diagonal, the less we are inclined to call it research in AI. Clearly, the progress in chess theory (which moves along the HCK axis) can hardly be regarded as part of AI, because of its lack of MCP. Likewise, we think that a certain minimum amount of human-compatible knowledge is required for a computer program to qualify as AI. Along this dimension, the development that has led to Deep Blue, in our opinion, is at the lower border of AI research, if not beyond.

The example of chess shows us that research has split into two streams: One that proceeds close to the HCK axis and is concerned with a deeper understanding of human problem solving and the domain knowledge on which it relies. The other stream is concerned with the development of faster and better algorithms and hardware heading for an exhaustive search. The little work that has been done in the white area in between has only been moderately successful in terms of our combined measure. We believe that this divergence can also be found in many other areas of AI like, e.g., Machine Learning or Natural Language Understanding.

Apparently, progress along the axes faces less resistance than progress along the diagonal. The question is "Why?".

4.4.5 A Hypothesis on Research Effort

We interpret Fig. 4.2 in the way that moving towards a better model (in terms of the overall value defined above) requires more effort if this improvement in value is made along the diagonal than if one proceeds along one of the axes. We think that the effort that is necessary to proceed a step along one axis is proportional to the progress that has already been made along the other axis. Only in the special case of a research program that proceeds along a single dimension (as e.g. the research in computer chess) will the increase in effort be proportional to the increase in value. This leads us to the following hypothesis:

The total effort that has to be spent on an AI problem is proportional to the product of the values along the axes HCK and MCP.

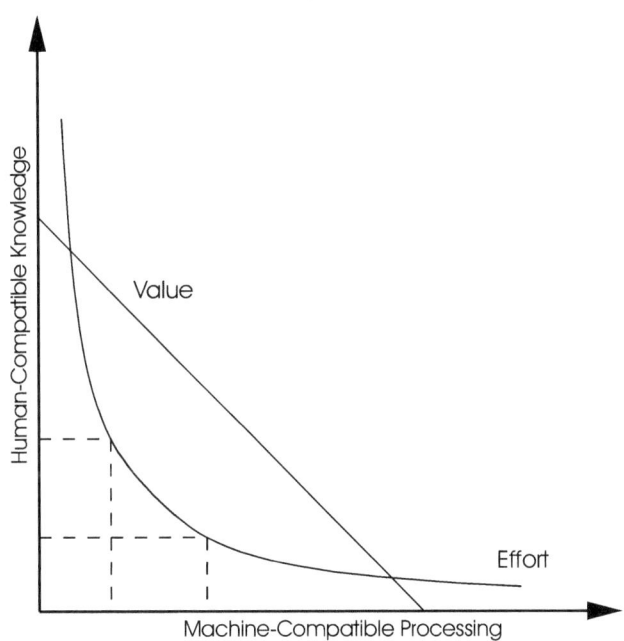

Fig. 4.3 The discrepancy between a class of models that are equal in effort and a class of models that are equal in value.

As an illustration consider the curve depicted in Fig. 4.3, which shows a line of AI problems which require the same effort, i.e., problems for which the area of the rectangle spanned by the co-ordinates is constant. We believe that the status quo of AI research could be described with such a curve. Relatively few progress has been made along the diagonal, while considerable progress has been made along the axes. On the other hand, consider the line which depicts a class of AI models sharing the same overall value. According to our hypothesis, there is a noticeable discrepancy between these two graphs, i.e., there is a difference between the value of an AI model and its required effort.[78]

From these deliberations, it follows that HCK and MCP cannot be treated independently. A possible way how they are interrelated can be derived within the theory of semantic networks. This theory seems adequate for this task, because, on the one hand, semantic networks are a psychological

---

[78] Note that this curve is not equivalent to the well-known search vs. knowledge trade-off studied, e.g., in (Berliner, Goetsch, Campbell & Ebeling, 1990) and (Junghanns & Schaeffer). For example, perfect endgame databases are used in many playing programs. They provide a maximum amount of knowledge with no search. However, the knowledge contained in these databases is not very human-compatible, as can be seen from the hard time that various endgame specialists had in understanding and extracting playing strategies from such databases (Roycroft, 1988), (Nunn, 1994). On the other hand, they are very machine-compatible: a simple database lookup suffices for perfect play. Hence, we would plot such approaches with low HCK, but high MCP values, at about the same spot where we would put programs that play such endgames using brute-force search.

model of human memory organization and, on the other hand, several variants have been successfully implemented and had a considerable influence on AI research.

A semantic network consists of nodes and links that connect such nodes. The nodes are to be understood as representations of basic concepts like objects or properties, whereas the links represent relations between these concepts. The resulting structure is a model of human semantic memory organization. Processing in such a semantic network is guided by the links (either in the form of explicit rules or by spreading activation, i.e., a sufficiently activated node spreads some of its activations to its neighbors, which in turn may receive enough activation to spread out). When there are sparse links between nodes that form a linear and mostly hierarchical structure, computation will be quick and easy. When the link structure is dense and cyclic, computation becomes problematic due to circularity and to the exponential growth in the number of possible paths. Thus processing depends on the number and the structure of the links in the network.

Classical semantic memory models[79] rely on the power of hierarchical, sparse network structures, but there is strong critique on this situation. Klimesch argues that these conceptions are misleading and he shows that they contradict important experimental data (Klimesch, 1994). He instead pleads for highly interconnected and cyclic memory structures in the following sense: The more connections a concept is associated with, the more meaningful is that concept. The expert who really understands what he is doing and who can apply his knowledge in most different situations has a much more interconnected memory structure than the beginner who just learned some strict rules. The interesting thing is that human memory performance becomes better and quicker with increasing connectivity of concepts, which is exactly the reverse for computational processes.[80]

While our discussion on the trade-off between HCK and MCP has been mostly qualitative, we believe that in the formalism of semantic networks it is possible to define operational measures for HCK and MCP on the basis of the network topology: HCK is high when the link-to-node ratio is high as in the interconnected and cyclic structures of human semantic memory. On the contrary, MCP is high when the node-to-link ratio is high as it would be the case in sparse and linear structures that are suitable for computer processing. Such a construction makes the interrelation of the two axes explicit and directly supports the product law we postulated.

4.4.6 Steps towards a Re-unification of AI

We take the quotation preceding our paper as an intuitive definition of the goal of AI. The goals expressed in this statement are on the one hand to produce intelligent behavior in the form of a

---

[79] E.g. (Collins & Quillian, 1969), (Anderson, 1976).
[80] One of the authors made extensive experience with this and other facets of problematic computability of interconnected structures when simulating Klimesch's model in his diploma thesis (Winkler, 1991).

"successful chess machine" and, on the other hand, to "penetrate to the core of human intellectual endeavor". However, the development of AI research, in particular in the domain of chess, has shown that the latter is not an immediate consequence of the former. Achieving functionality does not necessarily increase the understanding of how we achieve this functionality. We think the original motivation of research in computer chess, namely "merely" to build a successful chess machine, has to be replaced with different goals that require a reconciliation of machine-compatible processing with human-compatible knowledge. However, according to our hypothesis, we cannot expect this to be easy (if possible at all). In the following we would like to give a few examples for rewarding and challenging tasks in the domain of computer chess.

A very rewarding task would be the development of a computable vocabulary of chess concepts in which chess knowledge can be formulated. The characteristics such a representation formalism has to incorporate are that it has to be sufficiently expressive for formulating abstract strategic concepts, that it has to be extensible and can be easily understood by a user (HCK), and that it can be efficiently implemented (MCP). The need for such formalisms has been recognized early in computer chess research. In (Zobrist & Carlson, 1973) an advice-taking chess program is described which aims at allowing a chess master to "advice" a playing program in terms of this language. Many formalisms have subsequently been developed in the same spirit (Bratko & Michie, 1980), (George & Schaeffer, 1990), most of them limited to certain endgames.[81] A recent promising step into the right direction can be found in (Donninger, 1996), which introduces a very efficient interpreter of an extensible language for expressing certain characteristics of a board position. However, the expressiveness of the language is currently limited to propositional logic, a trade-off that had to be made because of efficiency considerations and the ability to provide a graphical interface that also allows untrained users to formulate rules.

Another promising field for further research could be the discovery of understandable knowledge in chess endgame databases with the goal of enriching chess theory. Consider, for example, Ken Thompson's impressive work on five-men endgame databases which is now publicly available on three CD-ROMs. The use of these disks allows chess programs to perfectly play the encoded endgames. However, many of these endgame databases are not thoroughly understood by human experts. The most famous example are the attempts of grandmasters to defeat a perfect KQKR database within 50 moves or the attempt of an endgame specialist to defeat a perfect database in the "almost undocumented and very difficult" KBBKN endgame (Roycroft, 1988). GM John Nunn's effort to manually extract some of the knowledge that is implicitly contained in these databases resulted in a series of widely acknowledged endgame books (Nunn, 1992), (Nunn, 1994b), (Nunn,

---

[81] See (Michie & Bratko, 1991) for a bibliography.

1995), but Nunn readily admitted that he does not yet understand all aspects of the databases he analyzed (Nunn, 1994a). It would be rewarding to develop algorithms for automatically discovering playing strategies for such endgames.[82] A particularly hard problem is that human-compatible strategies are typically simple, but not necessarily optimal in the sense that they require a minimum number of moves. For a machine, it is non-trivial to decide which suboptimal moves contribute to some global progress (and are thus part of a useful strategy) and which suboptimal moves do not improve the position. An attempt to automatically discover a simple playing strategy for the KRK endgame might easily produce the simple strategy "always move your rook away from the enemy king" which will always result in a won position (at least for the next 49 moves), but clearly make no progress towards the goal of mating the opponent's king. Other tasks that could be automatized include the discovery of opening theory mistakes, the automatic detection of particularly promising or unpromising line-ups or middle-game plans in certain types of openings, and many more. One can even imagine facilities that support tournament preparation by analyzing game databases with the aim of unearthing characteristics of the style of individual players and for studying their weaknesses and strengths.

Another obvious point, where chess knowledge would be of considerable importance, and probably the point with the highest commercial potential is the use of high-level chess knowledge in educational chess programs. For example, imagine a program that analyzes a certain position or an entire game on an abstract strategic level, tries to understand your opponent's and your own plans, and provides suggestions on alternative ways to proceed. Some commercial programs already provide such capabilities, but at a very preliminary level that usually is only able to detect tactical, but not strategic mistakes. The ICCA has recognized the potential of such programs, and has created *The Best Annotation Award* which will be awarded annually for the best computer-generated annotation of a chess game.[83] However, the competition suffers from a considerable lack of participants. Some preliminary work on using case-based reasoning for a strategic analysis of a given chess position can be found in (Kerner, 1994) and (Kerner, 1995).

Last but not least, we also believe that additional knowledge can increase the playing strength of current chess programs. However, the motivation to investigate such approaches has significantly declined with the somewhat unexpected success of brute-force programs. We have already illustrated the weakness of brute-force chess programs in certain endgame positions that require abstract problem-solving and chess-specific knowledge. For some preliminary ideas incorporating strategic long-term knowledge into conventional chess programs see (Kaindl, 1982), (Opdahl & Tessem, 1994), and (Donninger, 1996). However, we are also of the opinion that some of the early

---

[82] See (Muggleton, 1988) for some preliminary work.
[83] See ICCA Journal 15(4):235-236, 1992.

approaches to selective search need a re-evaluation in the light of the development of AI in the last 25 years.

4.4.7 Conclusion

Our description of research in AI, in particular in the chess domain, made use of two axes, human-compatible knowledge and machine-compatible processing. In this framework it became apparent that AI research has diverged into two streams that proceed along these axes, while we believe that the core of AI lies along the diagonal. For us, the reason for this development is that the effort for combining both aspects is considerably larger than for one-dimensional endeavors, and we have offered a hypothesis on research effort that could explain this observation. It follows that these aspects cannot be treated independently, if one wants to make progress along both dimensions.

The development that led to the Deep Blue vs. Kasparov matches, to the first game that a machine won against the human chess world champion in 1996, and finally to its first match win in 1997, in our opinion, demonstrates that proceeding along the "engineering" axis only, hard as it certainly has been, is comparatively easy. While Computer Chess has played a pioneering role in demonstrating that intelligent functionality can be achieved without a deeper understanding of how humans achieve that functionality, we think that it is time for moving towards a re-integration of the cognitive and engineering branches of AI and that computer chess provides a rewarding set of challenging problems that lead into that direction.

4.5 Summary

Using the example of chess programming, it has been shown that computation and meaning cannot be treated separately, because they obey spacetime holism's duality relation. The practical consequences for the field of artificial intelligence have been discussed.

5 The Representation Problem[84]

Contribution to the Thesis
The representation problem forms the center of the thesis. It is introduced by the use of a two aspect scheme, which relates to space and time structures and therefore makes the concepts of spacetime holism directly applicable. The suggested account of the representation problem is based on the notions of overlapping systems and of embedding, which have already been introduced in chapter 2. It is shown how mental representations can be meaningful for the cognitive system, and how a straight-forward realization of the suggested concept of representation leads to endless recursion, quite in line with spacetime holism's fundamental assumptions.

5.1 Two Aspects of Representations

What I am trying to summarize as the representation problem in cognitive science, is, indeed, a wide spectrum of problems. As a first approach, I would like to introduce a two aspect scheme.

Representations are identifiable states of a cognitive system that

- **refer to states of the system´s environment and**
- **are processed by the cognitive system.**

Before developing spacetime holism's account of the representation problem, I will use this two aspect scheme as a basis for the description of the most important viewpoints in cognitive science.

5.2 Representationalism and the Computational Theory of Mind

Very roughly, the computational theory of mind[85] is the belief in the appropriateness of the information processing paradigm for the study of cognition. It supposes that there is a designated, irreducible *symbolic* level of description characteristic of intelligent systems. Cognition is understood as the computation of meaningful symbols. These symbols are physically realized;[86] it does, however, not make any fundamental difference whether they are realized in biological cells or silicon chips. In this understanding of cognition, the notion of the symbol directly represents the two aspects; the symbol is supposed to mean something, and is the causal basis of computation.

As an engineering science, the computational theory of mind is named artificial intelligence (some critics call it nowadays GOFAI - "good old fashioned artificial intelligence"). Even the strongest critics have to admit that its strategies to build and program machines that solve intelligent tasks

---

[84] The general approach to the representation problem presented in this chapter has been published in (Winkler, 1999).
[85] A related notion is *cognitivism*, which is rather used in the context of psychology, where it means the opposite of *behaviorism*.
[86] Physical symbol systems hypothesis (Newell & Simon, 1976).

have been very successful, at least in some domains. There is, however, a philosophical part of the story, which raises crucial questions, and which deserves a closer look, therefore.

The computational theory of mind can be regarded as a combination of an account of reasoning and an account of mental states. Behind the account of reasoning stands, of course, the notion of computation, behind the account of mental states stands *representationalism*. The two work together in the following way.

Computation, which is per definition only sensitive to the syntax, is supposed to conserve the semantic content. Once a given problem has been formalized in an appropriate way, the syntactic processing will not do any harm to the meaning, which is at the beginning laid into the symbols.

It is easy to see what kind of understanding of the terms semantics (or meaning) stands behind this approach. A symbol means something to an external observer (or designer) of a system, who sees both the state of the system (the symbol) and the state or entity it refers to. Using the notions of spacetime holism, semantics can only be an outside observer's matter, there is no way of believing that the symbol means something to the system.

A related notion is intentionality, which is treated in the computational theory of mind as follows. For a cognitive system, to hold e.g. a belief or wish means to be in a functional relation (believing, wishing) with the symbolic representation of a possible state of affairs, e.g. "the weather will be fine tomorrow." The intentional state, i.e. the functional relation, inherits the semantic value of the representation it refers to.

More generally, intentionality expresses the "aboutness" of mental states.[87] One of the major problems of representationalism is given by the question that concerns the status of the "thing" a mental state or representation is supposed to be about. E.g. we, as human cognitive systems can have mental states that are about things that "do not exist." Instead of going into the details of this discussion, I will give spacetime holism's account of this problem in 6.5.

5.3 The Critics of Representationalism

As a very broad and explicit approach, the computational theory of mind is an invitation for all sorts of critique, from technical to philosophical ones. Not every critique is fundamental, and much debate concentrates on parts of the theory, e.g. whether the meaning of representations can be learned or is inborn. There are also different degrees of believing in the computational theory of mind (strong versus weak understanding of artificial intelligence).

---

[87] (Brentano, 1874)

In this place, I am interested mainly in fundamental arguments, and I chose what I think are the three most important adversaries of representationalism, namely connectionism, autonomous agents, and radical constructivism.

5.3.1 Connectionism – the Sub-Symbolic Paradigm

While the focus of traditional artificial intelligence is on higher levels of intelligence (e.g. language, game playing), connectionism concentrates on low level processes like perception and associative reasoning. In this domain, there seems to be no justification for assuming a symbolic level of processing. Instead, the seemingly intelligent behavior is brought forth by the interaction of very simple (per se not intelligent) neuron-like units. Such neural networks show some aspects similar to biological cognition, e.g. learning and pattern matching, which are more or less ignored by the symbolic approach.

In terms of the suggested two-aspect scheme of representations, the two approaches differ significantly. While symbolic computation relies on the possibility to strictly separate syntax from semantics, the two are closely linked in connectionism: similar states mean similar things. The concept of the symbol, which forms the interface between syntax and semantics in representationalism, looses its fundamental, causal status and can be accepted only as a useful description for some higher level cognitive processes.

For the connectionist, there is a fundamental level of description other than the symbolic (it is called "sub-symbolic"). Cognition is understood as the outcome of the computations performed by a highly connected set of simple neurons whose states cannot be given a symbolic meaning.

By concentrating on the issue of learning, the relational aspect (the meaning) is no longer a mere designer's matter. The cognitive scenario for neural networks is that of a self-organizing system trying to adapt to an environment. The learning rules (whether supervised or unsupervised) adapt the parameters of the neuronal units such that errors are minimized.

Representational codes in a connectionist network are distributed – it is the activation pattern of a set of units that counts. Other than in the symbolic architecture, the loss of a part of the system not necessarily has a destructive effect on the performance of the whole system.

While there are significant differences between symbolic and connectionist approaches in the question how the cognitive system works, there seems to be no relevant difference in the general cognitive scenario: The cognitive system, at least as a whole, represents the environment it interacts with via information exchange. The external, relational aspect of representation is thus accepted by both the symbolic and the sub-symbolic approaches.

5.3.2 Autonomous Agents

The tension between the symbolic and connectionist approaches forms only a part of what can be understood by the representation problem. While symbolic computation and most of connectionism still agree on the usefulness of mental representations, there is strong critique on the representational view of cognition in general.

An important example is given by Rodney Brook´s work on autonomous agents. In (Brooks, 1987) he argues for the necessity to embody intelligence and to situate it in a real world. The usefulness of a representational level of description of the processes in the agent is rejected. From the two-aspect scheme this looks like a stress of the first, relational aspect and a fundamental critique of the second, computational.

While mostly for the representationalist, but also for the connectionist, the hardware does not really count, the concrete material in which a robot is built, however, does very well matter for autonomous agents. There is also a different cognitive scenario attached to the approach of autonomous agents. Without saying it this way, Brooks seems to take the system consisting of the agent and its environment in interaction very serious. These interactions can no longer be reduced to information exchanges as was the case in the traditional input-output scenario.

As a consequence of stressing the interaction system, the cognitive system as a unity receives a less important status. The central agency that seems to stand behind a cognitive system must be understood as merely emerging from the collaboration of a set of modules and the behaviors they are concerned with.

5.3.3 Radical Constructivism

Radical constructivism's fundamental critique of the assumption of mental representations[88] has many aspects. The most obvious one is the rejection of a given, objective reality. How can there exist representations when there is nothing that has independent existence? For a better understanding why constructivism and the assumption of representations do not fit together we take a look at Maturana´s concept of an autopoietic unit.[89]

In the context of autopoiesis, *organization* means a set of relations between the parts of a system that is brought forth by the system and is being maintained. The autopoietic organization of a biological cell can be regarded as *closed* in the sense that it is defined by the autopoietic unit itself, by its circular operations. We also speak of an *operational closure* of an autopoietic unit. The behavior of the parts of a unit is specified by the organization. It is meaningful only to the unit and

---

[88] (Varela, Thompson & Rosch, 1991)
[89] (Maturana & Varela, 1987)

serves exclusively for maintaining its organization. The "input" a unit receives from the environment is not regarded as meaningful or informational, but as a mere *perturbation* that is not instructive to the unit and its organization. Perturbations can thus be regarded as mere provocations for the system to switch to a different, self-determined state. From this it is clear that the behavior of the parts of the unit (respectively their *phenomenology*) does not *represent* anything from the environment.

From this analysis of the concept of autopoiesis, one is tempted to conclude that constructivism is not very much concerned with the relational aspect of the idea of mental representations, i.e. the interaction system with the environment. However, in later publications[90] one of the founders of autopoiesis stressed the role of embodiment and situatedness, quite in the sense of Brooks' autonomous agents. From the viewpoint of spacetime holism, this seems like a growing awareness of the limitations imposed by the restriction to hierarchies of autopoietic systems (see section 2.5).

In order to underline this critical point, I would like to make a destinction between two types of interactions autopoiesis is concerned with. On the one hand there are the cyclic operations in the autopoietic unit, on the other hand there are mere perturbations. The first do play a role in the organization, the latter do not. Perturbations are *structural interactions,* which means the exchange of matter and energy. We can say the autopoietic unit *is structurally open* but *organizationally closed.*

A critical question for the separation of *organizational closure* and *structural openness* is the treatment of meta-units. Maturana and Varela state reciprocal and relatively stable structural interactions between a unit and its environment *(structural coupling),* especially between two or more autopoietic units. This may lead to the formation of so-called 2nd-order autopoietic units (organisms) and even 3rd-order autopoietic units (societies). Having an eye on representation, we may ask which role the behavior of the parts of a unit might play for the meta-organization. It is important to show how Maturana solves this problem before formulating a critique.

For Maturana the parts of a unit do not play a specific role in the meta-organization. It is just the *organization of the unit* that serves the meta-organization. In such a case, the organization of the unit is more complex, but the parts of the unit still maintain the organization of the unit itself, and nothing else. Maturana´s example for this is the *egoistic altruism* of the antelope that leaves the group when lions attack and thus gives away its life for the others. The behavior of the antelope is regarded as *egoistic* because the antelope just fulfills its own autopoietic organization.

---

[90] (Varela, Thompson & Rosch, 1991)

I see two major problems with this view. The first is the unclear role of the perturbations between the lower-level units for the closed organization of the meta-unit. The second problem is given by the restriction to *hierarchical relations* between organizations - this one is much easier to argue: If we have to deal with overlapping cyclic organizations, the behavior of a part located in the (structural) intersection of these organizations cannot be understood as serving just one organization, it would help maintaining more than one organizations being specified by more than one organizations. Thus the inside of one cyclic organization could be specified by another organization. For sure, Maturana would not see overlapping cyclic organizations as autopoietic. But if we can show that dealing with them is inescapable, when it comes to higher-order systems, we have derived a serious limitation for autopoiesis.

In support of this, there is strong critique on the application of autopoiesis to social systems. For example, Hejl argues that social systems cannot be regarded as autopoietic units,[91] he states that every individual contributes to a set of social systems which destroys the idealized hierarchical picture.

While constructivism has a clear answer to the relational aspect of mental representations, namely complete denial, it is not necessary for a constructivist to deny the computational aspect as well. It would, indeed, be compatible with the central idea of constructivism to understand cognition as computation of *presentations*,[92] which are meaningful to the cognitive system that constructed them, but do not refer to some outside reality. However, constructivism's strong link to the theory of self-organizing systems suggests that such presentations are rather understood as emergent states, which do not play a primary causal role for cognition.

5.4 Spacetime Holism and the Representation Problem

Formulating spacetime holism's account of the representation problem is not much more than summarizing what has already been said. Beside the central features of spacetime holism the main building blocks are the shift to systems theory including the assumption of overlapping systems and the concept of embedding.

5.4.1 The Systems Formulation

Cognitive systems are inside observers constructing outside views. Talking of inside observation means that the interaction game between observer and thing observed can and should be regarded as some kind of system. Due to its account of part-whole containment, dynamical systems theory provides a useful basis to formulate spacetime holism's approach to the representation problem.

---

[91] (Hejl, 1994)
[92] This notion was used by Ernst v. Glaserfeld in a personal communication.

However, there are two overlapping systems that have to be taken into account. Beside the interaction system with the environment, the cognitive system itself must be regarded as a system as well – in a sense similar to autopoiesis. It is central to the suggested approach to the representation problem to acknowledge that these two systems are overlapping, which imposes a limitation to the applicability of the theory of self-organization. In the framework of spacetime holism, however, such system overlaps are unproblematic; the statements derivable from analyzing the two respective systems separately come together as aspects of description in the synoptical view.

5.4.2 The Cognitive Scenario

In the introduction to the representation problem at the beginning of this chapter, I pointed out two aspects of the problem, namely the relational and the computational aspects. The first has to do with the spatial relation between a cognitive system and its environment and the second one with the temporal relation between states of the cognitive system. From the viewpoint of spacetime holism these aspects can be identified with wave and particle aspects of cognitive processes that form a duality. It is impossible to make clear cuts, analyze the aspects separately and add them up again for a full understanding. The relational aspect between a cognitive system and its environment is in the last consequence incompatible with the computational aspect. Continuity in space and continuity in time cannot be fully present simultaneously. If a representation is to be processed merely by its local properties, it cannot mean something which requires non-locality in space. The two aspects belong to different description schemes. Yet, spacetime holism's conceptual framework allows the formulation of some elementary relations. Before I go into this, I have to introduce the cognitive scenario.

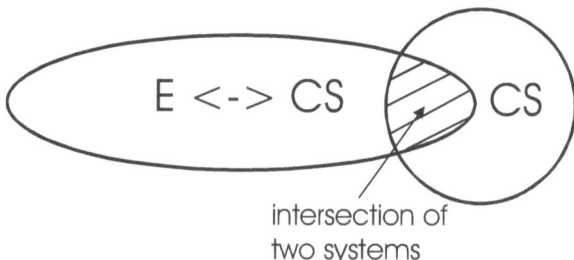

Fig. 5.1. The cognitive scenario consisting of two intersecting systems: the cognitive system CS and the system formed by interacting parts of CS and its environment E.

Fig. 5.1 shows the two intersecting systems involved in the cognitive scenario. First, the cognitive system whose operational closure is stressed by autopoiesis, and second, the interaction game between (parts of) the cognitive system and (parts of) its environment, whose status as a dynamic unit has been underlined in (Mandelblit & Zachar, 1988). Again, there is no problem for the presented approach, as both systems stem from in principle incomplete descriptions, or - to formulate it differently - a construction like this requires an assumption that forbids complete descriptions of parts or subsystems.

In the chosen scenario the representation problem has to be formulated as follows:

> In which way can one part, namely the cognitive system, both contain and produce phenomena of the whole system consisting of the cognitive system and its environment in interaction?

The general answer to this question is already given and only has to be repeated in this place: There is a duality between two aspects, the wave aspect being responsible for the containment of the (non-local) dynamics of the whole in each part, and the particle aspect being the pre-condition for treating the parts as entities that roughly can be defined in space, show some local causality and thus might be taken as producers of the system's dynamics.

In the following I will use spacetime holism's concepts for a more detailed analysis of the cognitive scenario.

According to the first fundamental duality relation, space and time are correlated in a specific way, which can be exploited for the (necessarily incomplete) extraction of some spacetime elements involved in the cognitive scenario.

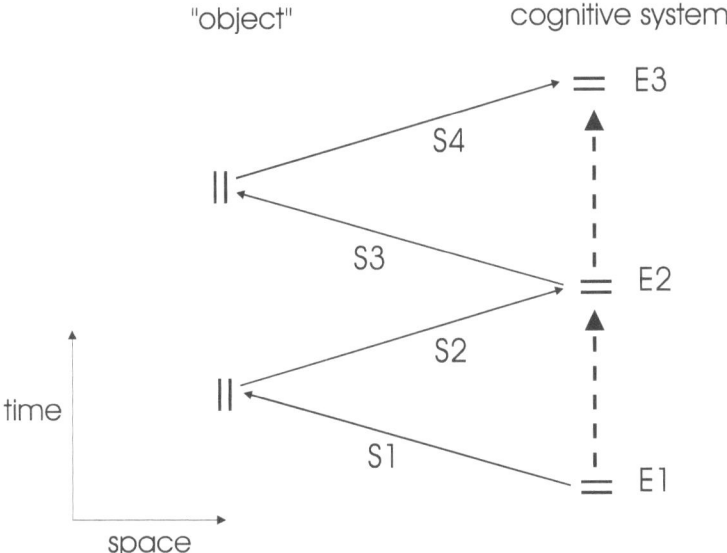

Fig. 5.2 The interaction game between an "object" and a cognitive system. The spatial discontinuities on the side of the object correspond via the signals S_i with temporal discontinuities on the side of the cognitive system (events E_i). The non-local structure of the whole system is mapped to the sequence of events in the cognitive system.

Fig. 5.2 shows how the spatially continuous signals S_i between "object" and cognitive system correspond with the temporally discontinuous events E_i in CS. On a higher level of abstraction, the spatially discontinuous object, which reacts to CS´s actions, corresponds with a continuous sequence of events in CS. The object, which for the outside observer is a mere spatial phenomenon, is accessible to the inside observer only by the internal temporal structure. The represented phenomenon, of course, is the spacetime pattern of the interaction game between the cognitive system and its environment and not the object as such.

What is the difference between an object and a cognitive system? Does the object represent the interaction game between itself and the cognitive system in the same way as the cognitive system does? The fact that some temporal structure can be observed on some entity does not suffice for making a distinction between object and cognitive system. There is something in addition for a cognitive system. Holding a representation of something means for an *inside observer* to *know* about his or her own next states and to be able to *force* specific sequences by acting on the object. The requirement for this ability is that an additional rotation of the spacetime structure takes place in the cognitive system (which is not illustrated): The temporal structure is mapped to a spatial structure within the cognitive system. This spatial structure becomes part of the whole system as *the particle aspect* of mental representations, it is this aspect that allows us to model cognition as computation of representations with some success. This additional rotation of the spactime structure taking place within CS can be understood as *implication* in the sense of David Bohm, and, of course, reflects the second fundamental duality relation between levels of abstraction.

As an example, think of the concept of an *obstacle*, which - for an outside observer - is an entity in space. For the inside observer (i.e. a cognitive system interacting with the obstacle) the obstacle can in the first place only be a set of temporal links between states of the cognitive system, e.g. "when I try to walk through, it will hurt". This temporal relation is the representation of the interaction game of the whole system in one of its parts, namely in the cognitive system. It is the wave aspect of the mental representation of the obstacle, which makes up the *meaning* of the representation. On the other hand, we can only speak of a computable representation of the obstacle, when the cognitive system is able to transform the temporal rule (walk->hurt) into an entity in some internal representation space. As an internal spatial entity the representation "obstacle" shows stability in time (it is memorized) and can be used as the basis for calculations that guide the behavior of the cognitive system (e.g. avoid walking through obstacles).

When trying to reduce mental representations to one side of the duality we are trapped in contradiction. Regarding representations merely as the temporal structure in the cognitive system allows the cognitive system to contain phenomena of the whole system and therefore to carry meaning. Yet, when there is only the wave aspect representations would loose their *effect* (see section 5.5) - there would be no influence of the representations on the cognitive processes. If we regard representations as purely spatial and syntactical structure, they can very well be understood as the causal basis for the cognitive processes, but can in no way carry meaning.

It is inconceivable to simply add wave and particle aspects in order to get a full picture. The two aspects stem from two different modes of description of the one spacetime whole and cannot be analyzed separately. As a consequence, attempts to solve the problem of mental representations under the paradigm of information processing are doomed to failure. Information only means something when being processed, information can therefore not be separated from processing.[93]

5.4.3 Representationalism's Hardest Problems

The two hardest philosophical problems for representationalism are the following:

- If the meaning of a mental representation is a relation to some external world, how can there be representations of "things that don't exist"

- In the first place, the semantic relation between a mental representation and some entity of the external world is an outside observer's matter. Can a representation be meaningful for the cognitive system?

Spacetime holism overcomes these problems, as is argued in the following.

5.4.3.1 "Things that Don't Exist"

To assume the intentionality of a mental representation means to assume that the mental representation is about something. This approach requires some kind of ontological status for that something. What, however, is the ontological status of things that don't exist?

For the radical constructivist, there are no representation and talk of intentionality is meaningless, therefore. The mental concepts are mere constructions serving the mental organization of the cognitive system. This is just one aspect of the story for spacetime holism. By regarding the interaction game with the environment as a system, as well, representations can mean something, respectively can be about something. The something a mental representation is about is in the first place not a thing out there, but a spacetime pattern of the interaction game. This statement already takes away a part of the problem of non-existent things.

There is, however, a second part, which has to do with the (necessary) simplification of regarding just two overlapping systems involved in the cognitive scenario. On a closer look, the cognitive system itself has to be understood as a mixture of overlapping systems in interaction. Even a

---

[93] See chapter 4

representation can be regarded as a system. From this picture, which is fully in line with the basic assumptions of spacetime holism, it is clear that mental representations, by interacting with each other, bring forth spacetime patterns that, again, are represented. Compared to the interactions with the environment, these internal processes are probably much more important.

The conclusion of this is, to make the point with an example, that the representation of a unicorn can be understood as a representation of the interaction game between the representations of the concepts "horse" and "has a horn."

5.4.3.2 Meaning for the Cognitive System

A crucial dimension of the representation problem, which is mostly ignored, though, is the question *for whom* there is a relation between representations and the environment of the cognitive system. In spacetime holism it is definitely more than a mere outside observer's matter who states a relation between an entity of the outside world and a representation in the cognitive system. This is made possible by spacetime holism's assumption of part-whole containment. The part, i.e. the cognitive system, contains the semantic relation and can therefore carry meaning. The following section shows a straightforward development of this idea.

5.5 Semantics, Meaning and Causal Effect[94]

Spacetime holism's account of mental representations can be analyzed from a traditional perspective. For spacetime holism, the following attempt to discuss the notions of semantics and meaning in the context of dynamical systems theory and computation can only be a limited logical game. This game, however, is designed to further support the understanding of the presented approach to the representation problem, and especially the concept of embedding. The infinite recursions that automatically arise and that are vicious from a traditional perspective, are unproblematic for spacetime holism.

5.5.1 Assumptions

The scenario under investigation consists of the *world (W)* and the *cognitive system (CS)*, both part of one universal physical system, looked at from the perspective of an outside observer.

Ignorant of spacetime holism in this place, I assume:

A1: W is a *causal*, physical system with CS as a part.

For further analysis we have to separate CS and W and regard them as two systems. This can be done without loosing anything by describing CS as a function mapping the states of CS and W to

---

[94] This section is based on (Winkler, 1995).

states of CS, and by describing W as a function mapping states of W and CS to states of W. This is based on the natural view of CS and W to be interacting systems.

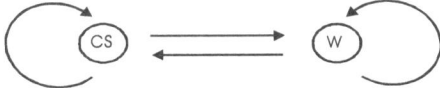

Fig. 5.3. CS and W interacting with each other and themselves.

5.5.1.1 Phenomena of a System

Before defining the approach to cognitive terminology the following should be clarified. We do not make any ontological assumption in addition to the physical system's assumption (A1). When talking of phenomena, representations, semantics and the like I talk of *observations*. The idea behind this is:

Whatever phenomena, representations, and semantics should be, they must be observable when regarded as parts of physical reality!

D1: A **phenomenon** of a system is an assertion an observer can make of the system in terms of the states of the system.

D2: An **effective phenomenon** of a system is a phenomenon of the system with some observable effect on other phenomena of the system.

If the observer can formulate an implication expression with the appearance of an observed phenomenon A as a nontrivial premise for the conclusion of the appearance of another observed phenomenon B, we call the phenomenon A effective for B. As outside observers, we would state a causal relation between A and B.

5.5.1.2 Mental Representations

I assume that the term *(mental) representation* is only useful when holding at least two properties.

D3/1: A representation is a phenomenon of CS.

Whatever specific properties else may be supposed for representations, they must be phenomena of CS alone, no observation of states of W is allowed to be part of them.

D3/2: A representation is an effective phenomenon for CS and W.

If we want representations to play a role for causal explanations of cognition, they must be effective for the states (and therefore for observed phenomena) of both CS and W, i.e. for *thinking* and *acting*.

5.5.1.3 Semantics

Semantics is a relation between a system's states and the states of some external system ("reality", truth, metaphysical ideas…). Having this and the distinction between inside and outside observation in mind in mind, we may define:

D4: Semantics is a phenomenon of the whole system made up of CS and W interacting with each other.

5.5.1.4 Meaning

Semantics is typically an outside observer's (or designer's) matter, who states (or creates) a certain relation between e.g. some bit combination of a digital computer and the temperature of a chemical process being controlled by the computer. The suggested understanding of the notion of meaning goes beyond that. There should be more to a meaningful state of a cognitive system than just an outside observer's statement.

In order to realize this, let us define the term *meaning* as the portion of semantics present in CS.

D5: A meaningful phenomenon is a phenomenon of CS holding semantics, consequently it must be effected by semantics.

5.5.1.5 Meaningful Representations

Now we can formulate an assumption on meaningful representations, which reflects the cognitivist approach to representation.

A2: Natural CSs, especially human thinking, have meaningful mental representations.

5.5.2 The Problems

The following two problems of self-reference are a direct consequence of the setup of the scenario and the chosen definitions.

5.5.2.1 CS as a Self-model

If CS holds meaningful representations as defined, it must contain knowledge of both W and itself, namely CS. Without additional assumptions, this contained knowledge of CS should contain knowledge of CS´s representations containing knowledge of W and CS and so on (Fig. 5.4). This is usually considered a vicious, as endless, recursion that has to be prevented. I think that this property of CS is essential, though: CS has to be a model of itself interacting with W rather than a model of W alone.

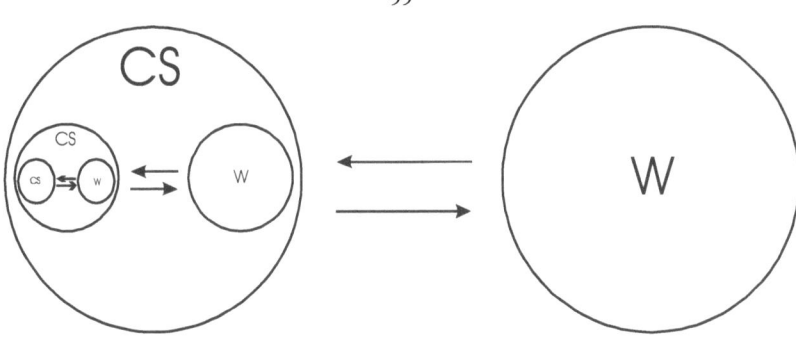

Fig. 5.4. Endless self-containment of CS+W in CS.

5.5.2.2 The Circularity of Effect

The effect of meaningful representations (on thinking and acting) is in general an effect on CS and W, therefore on semantics, which in turn has an effect on meaning and therefore on meaningful representations. One could try to avoid this circularity, but let us see where we get.

One popular assumption to deal with this self-referential infinity is that of successive loss of effect. It is based on the general assumption of convergent processes and used for theories of CS[95] and might be applied to CS-W interactions, as well. It is important to discuss it and to show its insufficiency.

5.5.2.3 Why Effect Does not Disappear

It is a nice property of many circular systems to converge towards some stable state or a permanently repeating sequence of interactions. Applying this view to the interactions in our CS+W system would seemingly solve the problem of infinite recursion. The closer the system´s states are to the stable solution, the less would be the effect of meaningful representations (via changes in the interactions of CS). The effect would disappear, when the stable state is reached. The first argument against this is that representations, according to the chosen definitions, should be both meaningful and effective, not either meaningful or effective or half meaningful and half effective. As a second argument I take the following implication of this view. Thinking and acting would take place for the only reason to make a given situation meaningful. When this is reached, thinking and acting would be caught in a loop or even halt, waiting for new things to happen and to destroy the meaning of the current situation. This would be a very poor role for CS - we know very well that this picture is inadequate.

---

[95] E.g. harmony theory (Smolensky, 1988).

5.5.3 The Dynamical Formulation

The circularity problem seems fatal, especially when not allowing circular processes to converge. The following attempt to deal with circularity is based on a closer look at time. Every interaction in the CS+W system takes place along the time axis. Let us see, how the endless recursion looks like when being resolved in time.

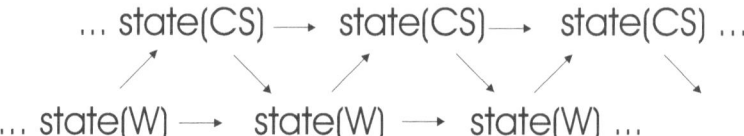

Fig. 5.5. The two interacting time sequences of CS and W.

Fig. 5.5 shows the two interacting time sequences of the states of CS and W. We are primarily interested in CS´s time sequence and ask, what the relation of this time sequence is to semantics. In other words: Can CS´s time sequence be meaningful? I think it can.

The time sequence of CS´s states is produced by CS and W interacting with each other and therefore has the capacity to hold semantics which is defined to be a phenomenon of the whole system CS+W. At the same time CS´s time sequence can be observed in CS alone, any possible assertion on the time sequence is a phenomenon of CS alone. It seems like we had candidates for meaningful representation, namely assertions on CS´s time sequence. But there is one essential postulate left for calling assertions on the time sequence of CS meaningful representations as defined: *the (observable) effect*. The crucial question is, how CS´s possible knowledge of the sequence of its past states could be effective for CS´s next interactions and therefore for semantics and meaning. Let me give an example to illustrate the problem of infinity and to give a (rather crude) idea how assertions on time sequences could have effect.

5.5.4 The meaningful computer

Imagine a computer (in our case CS) interacting with some environment (W), in our example a human user. We may regard the time sequence of internal states of the computer to be meaningful, but they are not accessible to the computer and cannot exert any effect. So let us add a routine to the computer program that protocols the internal states of the computer. This routine would perhaps detect that in case the user closes all open applications in a quick sequence the probability is very high for the computer to be turned off. As long as this knowledge does not change anything in the computer´s behavior, we are not interested in the routine - it would be a mere outside observer. But let us add a new kind of behavior to the computer program and have it being triggered by the routine. Now the computer would e.g. start displaying jokes from a database when calculating some probability that it is going to be turned off soon. Can we say now that the routine holds a meaningful representation? We cannot, because the joke-telling behavior of the computer changes the interactions between computer and user and therefore the meaningfulness of the computer´s knowledge of the time sequence. We would need an additional routine and, again, variations in the computer´s behavior. This necessarily is an infinite game when not allowing the interaction sequence between the user and the computer to converge towards a solution.

5.5.5 Dynamical Phenomena

A more serious treatment of the idea is based on the following definition of a dynamical phenomenon.

D1*: An (observed) dynamical phenomenon of S is an assertion an observer can make on S in terms of sequences of the states of S.

A very basic example for dynamical phenomena of a system would be the following. Imagine an oscillatory system containing a variable whose state regularly switches between 1 and 0. A possible dynamical phenomenon would be that a 0-state at time t-1 is followed by a 1-state at time t, another possibility would be that the time sequence 10101 is followed by 01, or that a 1 at time t-6 gives a 1 at time t. Dynamical phenomena of less deterministic systems could have degrees of probability, e.g. a sequence 110100 is followed by a 1 with a probability of 39% and by a 0 with 61%.

Replacing the term phenomenon with dynamical phenomenon gives us quite natural new definitions for semantics, meaning and meaningful representations.

Cs´s time sequence is supposed to be neither totally converging nor stochastic. This does not imply that there is no structure in it. Self-experience tells us that we can never be sure of what will happen in a given situation, but that we have quite good ideas of what could happen or what might have happened before. The suggested approach to meaning using assertions on time sequences seems to be a useful description of what we experience. We should not forget that everything we said is about observations and therefore has only descriptive character. This should also be kept in mind for the following extension of the idea - I call it *the engineer´s solution.*

5.5.6 The Engineer's Solution

A computer-apt version of dynamical meaningful representations might looks like this. The representations are (finite length) time-ordered lists of states of CS. Every part of such a sequence can been seen as a representation, too. The idea is to regard representations as sets of rules (one for every possible time cut) with the first parts as premises and the remaining second parts as conclusions, in the following sense.

If the time sequence of the premise matches the actual last states of CS, then try to act in a way that makes the conclusion time sequence really occur!

At every point in time CS computes the best matching rule and chooses its internal and external actions according to the implication of the winning representation. We can also think of compromises between a set of winning representations and of a lot of interesting variations, but this suffices for our purpose.

5.5.7 Why the engineer´s solution is not a solution

Of course, the engineer´s solution is only a description, or better, it is an implementation of a description, which bears the general problem of simulations - they are not of the same kind as the original. In this context we do not need much philosophical argumentation to show this, because we can use the above mentioned two problems to underline the insufficiency of the engineer´s solution. Self-containment and circularity require infinity, which has been shown even for observation and description. A computer cannot be infinite, not in the precision of its states and not in storage capacity, which the engineer´s solution would require a lot of. Therefore the computer cannot „contain" itself and not at all both itself and its environment.

5.6 The Chinese Room

The philosopher John Searle (1980) suggested his *Chinese room example* as a fundamental critique of the so-called *Turing test*.[96] Turing suggested to answer the question whether some candidate system is intelligent (and conscious) or not by studying its behavior: If we cannot tell the difference from the outside, then there is no difference. The background of this approach is the computational theory of the mind. The point Searle wants to stress in the Chinese Room example, in his own words, is that "semantics is not intrinsic to syntax."

> "Simply imagine that someone who understands no Chinese is locked in a room with a lot of Chinese symbols and a computer program for answering questions in Chinese. The input to the system consists in Chinese symbols in the form of questions; the output of the system consists in Chinese symbols in answer to the questions. We might suppose that the program is so good that the answers to the questions are indistinguishable from those of a native Chinese speaker. But all the same, neither the person inside nor any other part of the system literally understands Chinese; and because the programmed computer has nothing that this system does not have, the programmed computer, qua computer, does not understand Chinese either. Because the program is purely formal or syntactical and because minds mental or semantic content, any attempt to produce a mind purely with computer programs leaves out the essential features of the mind.[97]"

From the presented approach to the representation problem (and to cognition in general), there are several comments to make.

---

[96] (Turing, 1950)
[97] This is Searle's own summary of the Chinese room example in (Searle, 1992).

At first, there is full agreement concerning the impossibility to reduce semantics, meaning, understanding, intentionality, etc. to (per definition merely syntactical) computation.

However, there is a fundamental critique of the setup of the scenario. Unlike in the systems theoretical cognitive scenario, the interaction game between the Chinese room and its supposedly Chinese speaking environment is not regarded as a system. As a consequence, there is no relevant dependency of the "next input" from the current output. But it is essential to spacetime holism's account of cognition to regard a cognitive system in the context of the interaction game with its environment. It is not conceivable in spacetime holism to make a clear cut between the observer (in this case the user) and the cognitive system, as the room with its input-output window presupposes, without loosing anything.

Understanding, to make it very simple, means to know what comes next in the suggested approach. The attempt to build this feature into the computer scenario and its detrimental implications for computation have been analyzed in the preceding section.

Searle obviously accepts the principled conceivability of a full functional description of the behavior of a natural cognitive system as it stands behind the Turing test. This, of course, is impossible for spacetime holism from its very definition.

5.7 Generalizing the Concept of Representation

Before trying to put the presented holistic approach to the representation problem in cognitive science into a broader perspective, let me underline the role of the fundamental assumptions of spacetime holism that made the approach possible.

The most important contribution stems from the assumption of part-whole containment, which leads to a circle which is vicious only for a traditional worldview. As has been shown in section 5.5, such a circle is unavoidable, but meaningful in the context of the representation problem. The unity of space and time and, more specifically, the duality relation between space and time structure appears in the concept of embedding, which is borrowed from dynamical systems theory.

The link between the very general assumptions of spacetime holism and the cognitive domain was formed by a move to systems theory, especially the theory of self-organizing systems, whose limitations to disjunctive and hierarchical systems had to be broken, though.

In the form of the concept of representation, the basic assumption of part-whole relation should not only play a role in cognitive science, but seems to be applicable in a wide range of domains.

As a first example take *family therapy*,[98] where the relation between the patient´s psychic problems and the social system can be understood as a representation relation. The behavior of the patient and her or his inner conflicts represent the dynamics of the social system whose integrative part the patient is. Much of the systems dynamics can be read from the behavior of the patient alone, but the whole system is in need of therapy - the problems are irreducible problems of the social system.

Of course, it is not just the psychic (and psycho-somatic) problems that can be regarded as representations of social dynamics. Humans are highly social beings, therefore most of their behavior and mental life both reflects and produces social dynamics, and therefore represents the social system.

Another interesting example is art, whose understanding seems to reflect the respective culture. From a traditional understanding, a piece of art is a highly ordered structure meant to refer to reality or higher values like beauty, truth, God, etc., just like a mental representation ought to carry meaning. In a post-modern understanding, art lies much more in the eyes of the observer than e.g. in the painting. In addition to this, I would like to stress the social aspect of art perception and creation.

In some sense, the representation problem itself represents. On the one hand, the representation problem is related to all the problems of cognitive science, from philosophical to technical ones. On the other hand, a good account of the representation problem ought to be a building block for a cognitive theory. It follows from the suggested holistic approach, though, that we cannot expect a solution of this kind.

5.8 Summary

The representation problem and the known positions have been introduced by the use of a two aspect scheme which relates to spacetime holism's structural notions and to its concept of duality. The suggested alternative account of the representation problem has been developed by the use of the concepts of overlapping systems and of embedding. It has been shown how a mental representation can be meaningful for the cognitive system and how a straightforward application of the suggested account of representation leads to endless recursion, quite in line with spacetime holism's fundamental assumptions. It has finally been indicated that the holistic concept of representation might be useful not only in cognitive science.

---

[98] (Nichols & Schwarz, 1998)

6 The Hard Problem of Consciousness[99]

Contribution to the Thesis
It is shown that spacetime holism – unlike other worldviews - does provide a perspective to address the issue of consciousness in a consistent way. The approach is simple due to the fact that it adds only two assumptions to the conceptual framework (a fundamental "to be"-quality of the whole, and the phenomenon of "identification"), which can easily be linked to the basic structural notions.

6.1 Introduction

The holistic account of the representation problem introduced in the preceding chapter explains how phenomena of an interaction system involving the environment of a cognitive system are contained in a part, namely the cognitive system. By this, semantics, which is defined as a phenomenon of the interaction system, can be contained in the cognitive system and the mental representations can be meaningful. While this can be regarded as an important step towards a better understanding of cognition, there is one question still open - the issue of consciousness.

In this section, I suggest a solution to the so-called hard problem of consciousness, which is based on spacetime holism's treatment of the representation problem. The argument goes as follows.

I suggest that the reason for the obvious hardness of the hard problem of consciousness lies in two implicit assumptions characteristic of western thinking. The assumption of the fundamental existence of the object and the assumption of the fundamental existence of the self cannot both be valid, if something like a psychophysical link is taken for granted. Other than monistic approaches that are incompatible with one of the two assumptions, I strictly reject both assumptions. Spacetime holism, which in the first place is a view of the material world, can be extended by an assumption on the nature of consciousness, thus providing the basis for a non-reductive solution to the hard problem of consciousness.

6.2 Easy Versus Hard Problems

David Chalmers (1995) proposes a distinction between what he calls the easy and the hard problems of consciousness. While the easy problems concern possible scientific explanations of the structure and function of cognitive processes, the hard problem addresses the relation between conscious experience and the material world as it is described by natural science: Why are (some) physical processes accompanied by conscious experience?

---

[99] Spacetime holism's account of consciousness has been presented at the conference "Towards a Science of Consciousness" in Prague, July 2003.

In my view, Chalmers fully succeeds in showing that there cannot be a reductive explanation of this hard problem, i.e. the very fact of subjective experience cannot be explained on the basis of our structural and functional descriptions of the physical universe. However, this does not exclude the possibility of a non-reductive explanation. If we take consciousness to be fundamental, and if we can formulate a set of assumptions on the nature of conscious experience, which can consistently be related to our physical models, we may claim to have arrived at a satisfying scientific explanation of consciousness.

In the following, I will suggest a solution of this non-reductive kind which, however, significantly differs from Chalmers' approach.[100]

The starting point is a critique of two assumptions characteristic of western thinking: *the fundamental existence of the object (AFEO)*, and *the fundamental existence of the self (AFES)*. The rejection of AFEO, of course, is what spacetime holism is all about. The rejection also of AFES creates the possibility for an assumption on the nature of consciousness and a testable law relating scientific ("third-person") descriptions to phenomenological ("first-person") descriptions, quite in the sense of Chalmer's *psychophysical principles*.

6.3 Object, Self and Psychophysical Link

To make it clear from the beginning, I am suggesting a view of both mind and matter that radically differs from what is usually taken for granted in western thinking. For every such fundamental undertaking, it is good and necessary to criticize the ruling paradigms. This very often includes the danger of burning straw puppets, especially when no clear and generally accepted view of the domain exists, which is truly the case in both the philosophy of mind and the "philosophy of matter."

The following formulation of two assumptions (one on "matter" and one on "mind") is not meant to describe *the* common starting point for reasoning about consciousness, nor do I claim that these assumptions have never been questioned (in fact, every monistic approach to the mind-body problem is incompatible with one of them). What I am trying to say is that only a radical and rigorous rejection of *both* assumptions allows an integrated view of mind and matter.

6.3.1 The Assumption of the Fundamental Existence of the Object

In the classical, Newtonian picture of the material world, the universe is seen as a collection of particles interacting with each other, thereby obeying deterministic laws. The critique of this view

---

[100] Chalmers suggests to take information as the fundamental property linked to the existence of consciousness.

usually concentrates on determinism – according to the Kopenhagen interpretation of quantum theory, a kind of ontological non-determinism rules the behavior of matter.

There is, however, a second idea standing behind the classical worldview, which is much less questioned, namely the idea that matter comes in pieces (particles) that can be separated from each other (at least analytically), that exist objectively, and that can be defined to an arbitrary degree of precision, at least in principle.[101] Such a world would, indeed, be best described by a hierarchy of "right" models of different levels of abstraction (physics, chemistry, biology,…), where each but the fundamental level could be reduced to a lower level.

The worldview of spacetime holism explicitly rejects this picture and all of the listed properties of matter.

6.3.2 The Assumption of the Fundamental Existence of the Self

In the western philosophical tradition, as well as in folk psychology, the conscious self is understood as a closed entity, strictly separated from other selves. While the self may take a whole lot of different states, and while these states are influenced from the outside, the self, in its core existence, remains unchanged. Typical statements illustrating AFES are: "I try to discover my true self", "It is impossible to look into another person's self."

I am fully aware that rejecting AFES may face even more resistance than the rejection of AFEO. It is easy to see how essential the fundamental self is for "ourselves" (e.g. as the source of free will) and for any social system (responsibility for our actions).

However, I think it is mostly due to this "natural" assumption that there are so many unsolved philosophical problems centering around the relation between mind and matter.

When formulating an alternative, it should be stressed that rejecting AFES does not at all imply that conscious experience is taken as an illusion.[102] The eastern philosophical tradition provides a concept of an ultimate form of consciousness, called empty consciousness, which is void of any content and void of any self. This concept of consciousness underlies what I will call the fundamental "to be"-quality in section 6.4.1.

As a conclusion to this paragraph, let me try to answer the two above statements that were used to illustrate AFES. Self-discovery, i.e. the search for a "true" self, should be replaced by a notion like self-creation, i.e. the creation of more or less stable borders and differences to the outside world and

---

[101] Quantum theory and the theory of self-organization (including e.g. chaos theory) raise serious doubts of the adequacy of this picture.
[102] In a similar way, the rejection of AFEO does not imply that matter is taken as an illusion.

the maintenance of peaceful relations with our own past and future.[103] In a traditional understanding it is not possible to look into another person's self, but I would like to insist that it is very well possible to create a common consciousness (a common "self") with another person (empathy, love...), thus breaking the assumed closure of the individual self.

6.3.3 The Psychophysical Link

Both AFEO and AFES can be quite successfully criticized in their respective domains. However, the problems they cause are illustrated best when yet another "obvious" assumption is added, namely the assumption that there is a link between the worlds of mind and of matter. The following statements and questions underline the problematic relation between AFEO and AFES.

- *The same conscious subject exists on changing matter.*

- *The same piece of matter can in principle take part in different conscious selves (at least sequentially).*

- *What is the condition for a physical object or process to take part in the production of consciousness (two atoms of the same kind – one in my brain and one in a piece of cheese)?*

- *How can a high-level object (e.g. a human being) have a fundamental, irreducible consciousness, while it can be reduced materially?*

In the frustrating situation caused by the incompatibility of AFEO and AFES, it is the proposed strategy to weaken the status of both the self and the object, such that a reasonable psychophysical relation becomes possible.

6.4 Solving the Hard Problem

The approach of spacetime holism and the applicability of its concepts to systems theory puts us in the position to formulate an assumption on the nature of consciousness and its link to our descriptions of matter. Before doing so, I would like to stress that what I called the wave aspect is not per se an account of consciousness. The simultaneous connection between spatially distant parts (e.g. quantum entanglement, or the integration of distributed information in the brain (e.g. by means of oscillations, Crick and Koch 1990)) are surely important functional properties of conscious beings – function, however, cannot explain experience.

6.4.1 The "To Be"-Quality of the Whole

Spacetime holism grants a fundamental, ontological status to nothing else but to the spacetime whole. When taking the existence of consciousness serious, and when believing in a relation

---

[103] e.g. (Ford 1987)

between the material world and the world of conscious experience, there is only one reasonable option for a basic assumption on consciousness: There must be something like a fundamental experiental aspect *of the spacetime whole*. In order to express that this aspect does not have the properties standing behind the usual understanding of the term consciousness, this aspect is given the name *"to be"-quality*. Related notions are *empty being* or *filled nothing*.[104] Attempts to describe the "to be"-quality consist mainly of negative statements - most importantly, this elementary form of experience neither has a self nor an object, and it is even free of space and time concepts.[105] As a more positive description, the feeling of *unity* and of *being home* might be associated.

Quite analogously to the assumption of structural self-containment of the whole, the "to be"-quality is present everywhere in spacetime. By assuming an omnipresent form of consciousness, spacetime holism seems to be very close to panpsychism (or panexperientalism). The crucial difference is that for panpsychism every*thing* is conscious,[106] while in a fundamental sense only the whole is conscious for spacetime holism. Although the "to be"-quality is present anywhere in the spacetime whole, there are no well-defined parts that are conscious as such in the first place. For panpsychism, there is a difficult problem how the consciousness of one part mixes with the consciousness of another part to form a higher, common consciousness.[107] In spacetime holism this problem does not exist, at least in this form, - the question is rather why the spacetime whole *appears* to come in well-defined parts, both material and mental.

6.4.2 Compatibility of Descriptions ("Psychophysical Law")

On the one hand, spacetime holism provides a conceptual framework for an alternative description of the material world from an outside perspective. The basic notions have already been described: *continuity* versus *discontinuity*, *non-locality* versus *locality*, and the *duality relation* for spacetime structure.

On the other hand, there are introspective approaches describing different qualities of experience. Beside the assumption of the "to be"-quality of the whole, the assumption that both sets of descriptions, the external and the introspective, can be made compatible, creates a perspective for a scientific investigation of consciousness.

---

[104] c.f. (May 1989). The seeming contradiction between emptiness and fullness resolves as follows: The "to be"-quality is full in the sense that it comprises the whole spacetime structure; it is at the same time empty, because it does not make any distinctions and is therefor free of any categories and concepts.
[105] The categories space and time can be regarded as constructions: If there are no objects and relations, then there is no space; if there are no events and no causality, then there is no time.
[106] Panpsychism thus seems to subscribe to AFEO.
[107] c.f. (Seager 1995)

6.4.3 Identification

As the bridge between external description and conscious experience, a correlation between continuity (from a third-person perspective) and what is experienced as *identity* from the first-person perspective is assumed. Following from the structural properties postulated by spacetime holism and the assumption of compatible descriptions, there has to be a duality relation also for self experience.

The first side of this duality, the *spatial self*, depends on borders (discontinuities in space) and determinism (continuity in time). In this state we, as inside observers, are identical through time, as time is the continuous dimension. We loose this experienced quality when our borders are destroyed, or when the subjective, local causality of the chain of events breaks down (e.g. when we are shocked). The spatial self has a location in space, it makes a distinction between me and the world.

The second side of the duality, the *temporal self* makes a distinction between experiences and therefore between points in time. The temporal self is located in time. By giving up the spatial closure, i.e. by interacting, we get integrated with the world. The experienced quality of this kind of self is the feeling of identity with the world, as in this case space is the continuous dimension.

The two sides of the duality have to be regarded as just two aspects of self experience that usually do not take their extremes, and therefore do not exclude each other. While normal states of self-experience can be regarded as specific mixtures of both aspects (on different levels), the pure form of consciousness, which has been termed the "to be"-quality, can be re-introduced as full identification in space and time.

6.5 Representation, Intentionality and Qualia

Spacetime holism's approach to the representation problem has already been introduced in detail in the preceding chapter. Still from an outside view, representation is understood as the question in which way a spacetime pattern, which is produced by a system as a whole, can be contained in a part of this system. The *system* in the cognitive scenario consists of the cognitive system and its environment in interaction; the *part* is the cognitive system. By re-formulating it, this approach already includes a solution to the problem of intentionality. In the first place, a "mental representation" does not refer to an object in the world, but to a spacetime pattern of the whole system, whose part the cognitive system is.[108] The associated object does not even have to exist (to

---

[108] This scenario makes clear that the cognitive system is an inside observer. The externalization of a spacetime pattern as an object, to which the representation is said to refer, can be regarded as the crucial step for the creation of an outside perspective.

say it in traditional terms), for a mental representation can be a product of the interaction with other representations (see section 5.4.3.1).

So far, the concept of representation addressed relations in space. However, in a very similar way we can talk of memory as the representation of entities in time. Both forms of representation are central for a full-blown self attached with a high level consciousness (i.e. what is usually called consciousness). By representing, we create ourselves and the world by making a distinction, but at the same time we establish relations - the represented object is not me, but I know how to deal with it; the memory is not now, but it relates to what is now.

Representational processes can both be studied from a third-person perspective and from a first-person perspective. From the third-person perspective, we analyze their structure and function, from the first-person perspective, we experience different states of consciousness and different qualia.

As long as we understand that structural and functional descriptions can never be complete, we can cautiously use them to reason about the levels and states of consciousness attached to some investigated system or entity. As an extreme example, consider a rock, whose structural and functional analysis does not provide any reason for believing that it represents its environment or its history. We therefore conclude that it is not conscious in the usual understanding. This, however, does not contradict our general assumption of the omnipresence of the "to be"-quality. More interesting examples are different kinds of animals, whose more or less present cognitive and social abilities may lead us to draw conclusions e.g. about the qualities of pain they can experience.

This link between structure and function on the one hand and consciousness on the other must not be mistaken with the belief that the performance of a function is sufficient for the presence of consciousness.[109] The simultaneously present, different aspects of a system capable of representation require infinite complexity and self-containment. Therefore artificial (information processing) systems performing a definable, finite function can in principle not be conscious. The philosopher's pet in the consciousness debate, the zombie, is a hypothetical functional equivalent to a human being that lacks consciousness. From the suggested viewpoint, this construction simply does not work: There can only be functional equivalence to a human being, if the zombie has the same status as an infinitely complex and inseparable sub-structure of the whole. If so, it will have a full-blown consciousness as well.

6.6 Duality Between Inside and Outside Views

On the basis of the assumption of the link between outside description and inside experience a duality relation for inside and outside views can be formulated. It is the outside view that is built

---

[109] This is, roughly, Chalmers' suggestion.

upon discontinuities and cuts, while the inside view is connected to continuity and identification. Thus, the first duality relation between space and time structure immediately results in a duality relation also for the two types of observation.

It is interesting to connect the distinction between inside and outside views to developmental psychology.[110] When a baby is born, there seems to exist no difference between the self and the outside world, and also no difference between points in time. In the course of its development, the baby makes a sequence of cuts. The first cut is that between itself and the outside world. In other words, the baby's self and the world around it are the result of this cut. The second cut is that between objects (and other subjects) in the world, and on the inside the cut between mental states. This second step means, of course, nothing else than creating representations.

The duality between inside and outside views, both for space and time, can be given a geometrical meaning. Continuity, which from the outside appears as distance, is just one point from the inside view. As a first example, take the phenomenon of identification when e.g. watching a movie. The better the identification with the characters, the more the experienced distance to what goes on in the movie vanishes. An example for big distances from the inside perspective is given by time perception. For a small child, there is no link between "itself now" and "itself tomorrow," although the objective distance is not large. The child identifies more in space and less in time compared to an adult. For the child, tomorrow simply does not exist (or is infinitely far away).

Once again, I would like to stress the mixed nature of ordinary states of consciousness in this place. We are both inside and outside observers at the same time. When talking of a self there is not just an inside experience, but already an outside aspect which consists in regarding ourselves as objects in the world. There are most different levels of self experience and identification; in some respect, we identify not only with our body, but also with our belongings or territory, or with other people. The concept of representation presupposes such a mixture of self and non-self. In the first place, the object is different to me and thus not me, however, by representing the object it becomes part of me. In a similar way, internal states are both self and non-self at the same time: I can literally *be* the desire to achieve something, and I can look at this and other desires I have from a kind of outside perspective.

These considerations lead me to the question how the difference between self and non-self can be understood on the basis of the "representing" spacetime patterns of a cognitive system, or better, how self and non-self are constructed from these spacetime patterns. As an attempt to answer this question, I would like to introduce a distinction between the notions of *action* and *reaction*. A

---

[110] (Piaget, 1975)

spacetime pattern that strongly depends on other spacetime patterns would be reaction, a seemingly independent pattern would be an action.

Using this terminology, the self is the acting part, while the object has to react.[111] The self that has to react either does not feel well, or identifies with what it reacts to.[112] In a fully integrated system of identification, the distinction between action and reaction becomes meaningless – the system acts as a whole.

The asymmetry of the relation between spacetime structures will be a crucial step for the account of the passage of time suggested in chapter 7. Staying in the context of spatial relations, I would like to add another kind of spatial asymmetry, namely asymmetric containment. While in principle everything is contained in everything for spacetime holism, there are practical differences. We already had a difference between the subject and the object in the cognitive scenario: The subject represents (i.e. contains) the interaction game (including the object), while the object does not. Between selves, there are asymmetries both in the distinction between action and reaction and in the containment relation. These differences define social hierarchies.

What makes the structural asymmetries important for the issue of consciousness is the observation that the phenomenon of identification reflects this asymmetry by becoming directed. If there is identification between two parts, then it is stronger in the direction from the reacting, contained part towards the acting, containing part.

Along the time axis, the asymmetry defines the difference between past and future: We identify much more with the future that is not fully contained or represented in the now than we do with the represented past. An obvious example is the fear of death which has no counterpart in any feeling about our birth.

6.7 Summary

It has been shown that the worldview of spacetime holism does provide a consistent and simple perspective to address the problem of consciousness. Two hardly questioned background assumptions have been made responsible for the failure of known approaches, namely the assumption of the fundamental existence of the object and the assumption of the fundamental existence of the self, both of which are meaningless for spacetime holism. By lifting these assumptions, the world of conscious experience and the material world can be linked to each other by postulating a fundamental "to be"-quality of the whole and the phenomenon of identification,

---

[111] Konrad Lorentz (1973) describes the process of objectification, which e.g. is observed in the playing behavior of young dogs, as an attempt to learn how things react to different inborn actions (e.g. barking, biting, touching).
[112] Brainwashing techniques make use of this asymmetric identification.

which can be related to spacetime holism's structural notions, and which exhibits a duality relation. The concept of representation has played a central role for addressing the issue of qualia.

7 The Passage of Time[113]

Contribution to the Thesis
It is shown that spacetime holism – unlike other worldviews – does provide a perspective to address the problem of the passage of time. The argument is built mainly upon the concept of representation and the account of consciousness.

7.1 Introduction

The most fascinating of the riddles of time is the so-called passage of time which, however, is not accounted for by natural science. In this chapter, I suggest an approach to the phenomena of time which aims at explaining why time passes for us.

Conceptually, the passage of time has to be strictly separated from the asymmetry of time, the so-called arrow of time, which is a heavily discussed issue in natural science. This means that a possible scientific explanation of the arrow of time does not automatically explain why time passes. However, the suggested solution is based on asymmetric structural relations along the time axis. The decisive step, though, is made by bringing in the distinction between inside and outside observation[114] and the phenomenon of identification, exactly as formulated in chapter 6.

7.2 What is the Problem of the Passage of Time?

The problem of the passage of time is, maybe, best introduced by comparing two traditional views. For the ancient philosopher Heraclitus everything is in flux, while for his contemporary adversary Parmenides there is no becoming or vanishing. In the Heraclitean picture, flow is real, while the impression of flow is mere subjective and therefore illusory for Parmenides. Both views have their counterparts in the contemporary discussion of the passage of time.

It is taken as the message of relativity theory that the whole of spacetime must be considered as a kind of block that is simply given. Due to the relativity of simultaneity, there cannot be an objective flow of time, at least not as a physical phenomenon. This would contradict the principle of relativity which forbids physical effects that mark an absolute frame of reference. As long as the passage of time is seen as something non-physical, interpretations of relativity in the spirit of Lorentz are viable. For defenders of a Lorentzian interpretation, the saving of an absolute flow of time is one of the major motivations.

---

[113] Spacetime Holism's approach to the passage of time has been published in (Winkler, 2003).
[114] An kind of outside view of time is suggested by Price (1996). The integration with space misses, though.

As strong as the acceptance of the standard interpretation of relativity theory seems to be the rejection of its implications for the philosophy of time.[115] In physics, the case for a *re-temporalization of time* (countering Einstein's *spatialization of time*) is made by quantum theory and especially dynamical systems theory.[116] Notions like ontological randomness, unpredictable bifurcations etc. seem to fit a creative, dynamical view of time much better than a static spacetime block.

The situation of the current debate of the passage of time, both in physics and philosophy is, indeed, frustrating. I do not risk much by stating that the traditional worldview does not provide a perspective for a solution of the obvious contradictions and paradoxes around the passage of time, which I will introduce in the following.

The most intriguing aspect is that of time's motion. If time is moving (or if we are moving through time), there must be a speed. Speed, however, is measured as distance (usually, of course, a distance in space) per time. But what do we make of a speed that consists in a ratio time per time?[117]

A more sophisticated formulation of the paradoxical nature of time is presented by McTaggert,[118] who aims at showing the non-existence of the passage of time by the use of three meanings of time. What he calls the A-series expresses temporality in terms of past, present, and future. The B-series amounts to the relational order of events in terms of "earlier than", "simultaneous with," and "later than." The C-series represents the mathematical continuum of points dateable in clock time. While the B- and C-series reflect properties that do not change their validity, the properties of the A-series do change. Trying to relate the different series to each other shows no problem for mappings between B- and C-series, but the A-series causes considerable problems. One and the same event is as well past as it is present and future. In order to represent this, each point in time would have to contain its own order of all events, which is taken by McTaggart as a disprove of the existence of the A-series.

7.3 Spacetime Holism and the Asymmetry of Time

For a traditional worldview the asymmetry of time is a hard problem. There are on the one hand time symmetric micro-laws, while on the other hand the asymmetry of time is so obvious on the macro-level. For spacetime holism, this problem does not exist in this form, as any law has only approximative character. The spacetime whole can be supposed to be asymmetric along the dimension we call time in a similar way as matter is not symmetrically distributed in space.

---

[115] (Sandbothe, 1998)
[116] (Prigogine, 1984)
[117] The best one can do to overcome this problem in a straightforward way is the introduction of a second time axis (Franck, 2003).
[118] (McTaggert, 1908).

7.4 The Contributions of Spacetime Holism

One of the major differences between spacetime holism and David Bohm's holism is the treatment of time. There is no account of the passage of time derivable from Bohm's holism that adds anything to the frustrating situation in the physics and philosophy of time.[119] Rather, Bohm seems to presuppose a traditional understanding of a given flow of time.

The distinction between inside and outside observation, which has no counterpart in Bohm's holism, will play a key role for spacetime holism's account of the passage of time. The dilemma given by the opposing views of time's passage (real flow versus mere subjective impression) can be dissolved on the basis of the duality between inside and outside views.

Spacetime holism's attempt to construct consistent outside views, which already produced an outside view of spacetime covering the statements of relativity theory, has a strong implication for a possible account of the passage of time. It should be possible to explain the passage of time as an inside phenomenon, yet on the basis of the static picture presented in chapter 3.

Other essential parts of the fundament already laid by spacetime holism are the issue of representation, which can also be applied to time, the asymmetry of the containment relation, and, most importantly, the account of consciousness.

7.5 Infinite Complexity and Structural Containment

For the suggested approach to the passage of time, I have to take a closer look at structural complexity. I do so by asking a very general question: What are the possible relations between spacetime structures in different spacetime locations?

The concept of continuity already contains a first answer to this question. All spacetime locations along a line of continuity share some structure – in the case of spatial continuity they share a temporal structure, in the case of temporal continuity they share a spatial structure. As a general answer to the above question spacetime holism postulates that in principle the whole spacetime structure, which is an infinitely complex combination of both aspects, is fully contained in each spacetime location, which in turn can be regarded as part of the spacetime whole. What appears as a logical impossibility does make sense for infinite complexity; a finite structure cannot contain what it is part of. The radical assumption of full part-whole containment does, of course, not imply that some structural elements (patterns) could be measured equally well from all locations. As a consequence, an *asymmetrical relation of containment* for our necessarily finite descriptions of the infinite structural complexity can be defined. Asymmetry of containment means that some location

---

[119] The lack of a qualitative account of time in Bohm's philosophy becomes evident in a conversation between Bohm and the eastern philosopher Krishnamurti (Krishnamurti&Bohm, 1985).

A structurally containing location *B* is not contained by location *B* (relative to the same finite description).

The relation of containment can function as an ordering relation for a set of spacetime locations, e.g. location *A* contains location *B*, which contains location *C* etc. In such a chain, location *A* not only contains the structure of location *B*, but in a recursive manner also the structure of location *C* etc.

This chain of recursive containment is just an extension of the asymmetries I already suggested for spatial structures in section 6.6. It also should be mentioned that this chain of recursive containment is exactly what McTaggert's proof of the non-existence of time ended up with. For a traditional worldview, the infinite self-containment standing behind this idea is impossible. For spacetime holism, there is no problem - quite to the contrary, infinite self-containment is one of spacetime holism's fundamental assumptions.

7.6 How Time Passes

Let us now apply the conceptual framework to the analysis of the passage of time for inside observers. First of all, we have to understand that – from an outside view – an inside observer is a roughly definable spacetime structure which is extended along one dimension and more or less limited and closed along the other dimensions ("world tube"). By no other fact than this, the first dimension becomes the time dimension and the other dimensions become the space dimensions; for the ideal outside observer, there is no a-priori difference between these dimensions, there is just a dominant orientation of spacetime structures in a certain region of spacetime.

The assumption of identification explains why the inside observer experiences unity along the mostly continuous time dimension. As inside observers, we identify with "ourselves in the past" and with "ourselves in the future". What is an extended structure for the outside observer, thus becomes a single point (the self) for the inside observer.

Now, the recursive containment relation comes into play: If we assume that the time locations of the extended spacetime structure of the inside observer are ordered with respect to containment, we can say that each of these locations (moments) structurally contains the sequence of locations in one direction, while not or much less containing the sequence of locations in the other direction. By this, the first direction becomes the past, while the second becomes the future.

Along the inside observer's spacetime structure, in each point in time a full history of "memories" is contained (i.e. potentially *present* for the inside observer), part of which (the *self*) the inside observer feels identical with. While there is just one representation of the self in the recursive history of memories, there are many representations of every past experience in each moment. We do not only remember an experience, but we remember remembering the experience, and remember remembering remembering the experience etc., as well.

I think that our double nature as inside and as outside observers (i.e. as observers who construct an outside view), together with the postulated recursive history of memories, can explain our impression that time passes. On the one hand, as inside observers, we insist on the point-like nature of the self in time (i.e. the now); on the other hand, as outside observers, we associate an experience (or better: all memories of an experience) with a unique and unchanging point in spacetime (i.e. an event in the constructed spacetime block). These two points, the now and the event, have different experienced time distances at different moments: A deeper recursive memory structure means more distance, a shallow recursive structure means less distance, no recursive structure means no distance.[120] Two points that change their distance cannot be at relative rest. It seems to be our conclusion, therefore, that the two points must be in relative motion. When focussing on the outside view, we would say that the event is at rest while the now is moving. When focussing on the inside view, we would say that the now is at rest while the event is moving.

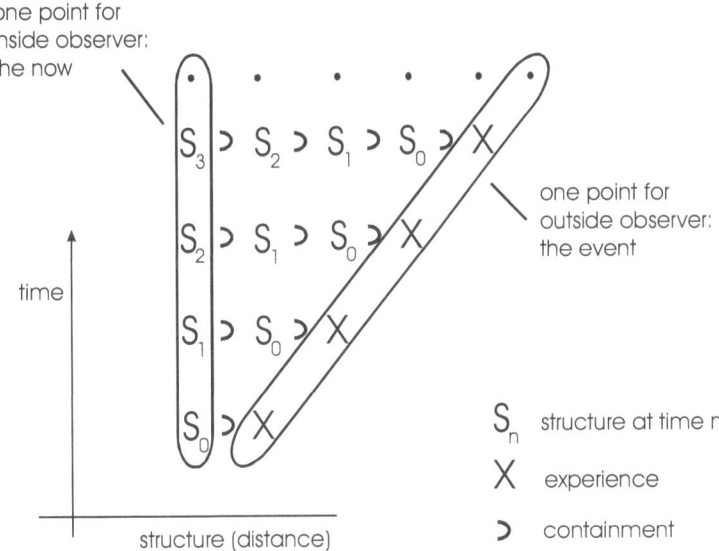

Fig. 7.1. Schematic illustration of an inside observer's spacetime structure at different moments in time. The recursive depth of the memory of an experience X defines the perceived temporal distance between the now and the experience.

Fig. 7.1 is an attempt to illustrate the argument on the passage of time. At different points in time the spacetime structure of the inside observer (S_n) contains recursive memories of an experience X

---

[120] Note that relative time distance and order are thus defined without reference to the outside notion of clock-time.

of different depths. According to the assumption on inside observation, part of the extended spacetime structure is experienced as one point in time (the now). There is, however, yet another point in time experienced: As partial outside observers we identify all memories of the experience X with a single event. It should be noted that the structure S_3 contains the whole structure of the diagram. What is drawn as identifications of two sets of temporally distributed structures can therefore be understood as local phenomena taking place in S_3 alone.

7.7 Summary

The suggested approach to the problem of the passage of time is mainly built upon the concept of representation, which is applied to the time dimension, and the account of consciousness. In order to cope with the phenomena of memory, a (representational) containment relation has been postulated that is not only asymmetric, but also recursive. In addition to this containment relation, the suggested explanation of the subjective impression of the passage of time is based on the distinction between inside and outside views. It is our double nature as inside and outside observers which makes both the *now* and the *event* single points in time. The contradiction following from this demands a construction like the passage of time.

8 Conclusion

The general purpose of this thesis has been the elaboration of the worldview of spacetime holism. More specifically, a solution to the representation problem of cognitive science, which reflects all the critical issues of the "world view problem," has been suggested.

The worldview of spacetime holism has been defined in equidistance to the involved scientific disciplines on an abstract level by the use of a minimal conceptual framework. I would like to summarize the thesis by underlining the role of the basic concepts for the main parts of the thesis.

Inside versus outside views
The distinction between inside and outside views does not only form the starting point for spacetime holism, it also appears as an end point. The suggested account of representation contains a perspective to explain how outside views are constructed from inside observation. The fundamental assumption of identification, which opens the door for the inclusion of consciousness, is directly linked to the inside view. However, the suggested understanding of "normal" states of consciousness as well as the suggested understanding of the passage of time are based on both inside and outside views or, better, on the interplay of both aspects. By this, the distinction between inside and outside views suffers the same fate as all distinctions in spacetime holism: in the final consequence it has to be dissolved.

Besides its potential to make the phenomena of consciousness accessible, the distinction between inside and outside views has been shown to be a very "practical" means to access the problems in the philosophy of science and in epistemology.

In addition to that, the clear conceptual distinction between inside and outside views has been the basis for the formulation of the Euclidean interpretation of relativity theory.

Spacetime integration
It has been one of the aims of the chapter on relativity theory to show that the relation between space and time is much simpler than suggested by the standard interpretation. However, the issue of spacetime integration is not just a matter of theoretical physics, but is maybe the most revolutionary of all the assumptions of spacetime holism, bearing the strongest consequences. Lifting the fundamental distinction between space and time means that the same structural notions can be applied to space and time. By this, it has become possible to radically reformulate the problems that are so critical for a successful scientific worldview (e.g. the problems inherent in the theory of self-organization).

The duality relation between space and time structure

There are, indeed, perspectives for proving the impossibility to fully separate space and time. Whenever a duality relation between space and time structure can be found, the involved spatial and temporal entities can in no way be regarded as independent of each other, and therefore cannot be assumed to be fundamental. Throughout the thesis, several duality relations have been suggested, namely the very general duality between particle and wave aspects which allows a foundation of the theory of self-organization, the duality between meaning and computation in AI modeling, and the duality between two aspects of self-experience.

Self-containment and infinite structure

Though the suggested account of representation makes use of all of spacetime holism's basic concepts, the assumption of self-containment (exemplified by the concept of embedding) plays the key role. Its link to the assumption of infinite structure has been illustrated in section 5.5 (Semantics, Meaning and Causal Effect), where it has been shown how a straightforward application of the concept of representation leads to endless recursion.

The consequences of the assumptions of self-containment and infinite structure are far-reaching. When the part contains the whole, the idea that the whole can be reduced to the causal behavior of in principle fully describable parts looses its basis. As a qualitative way to cope with this situation, the notion of "overlapping systems" has been suggested, which allows the part to contribute to and to be influenced by an infinity of different system contexts.

Representation

It could be argued that spacetime holism's concept of representation, which has been elaborated in the domain of cognitive science, is just a specialization of the general assumption of part-whole containment. As this feature is essential for the theory of self-organization, representation may, indeed, be understood as a very broadly applicable concept, which could only be indicated in the thesis.

It has been shown, though, that the account of representation makes it possible to extend spacetime holism. By the concept of representation and by the assumption of identification, spacetime holism can cope with the problems of consciousness and of time.

Identification

The assumption of identification, which links the concepts of continuity and of inside observation with subjective experience, is a small step for spacetime holism. By giving consistent accounts of the hard problem of consciousness and of the problem of the passage of time on the basis of this assumption, the worldview of spacetime holism has gained explanatory power where traditional worldviews fail.

References

Alexandrov, A. D. (1996). "On the principles of relativity theory," Classics of Soviet Mathematics, A. D. Alexandrov, Selected Works, **4**, 289-318.

Anderson, J. R. (1976). Language, Memory, and Thought. Lawrence Erlbaum Associates, Hillsdale, NJ.

Atmanspacher, H., et al. (1992). "Complexity and Meaning in Nonlinear Dynamical Systems," Open Systems & Information Dynamics **1**, 269-289.

Atmanspacher, H. (1993). Die Vernunft der Metis – Theorie und Praxis einer integralen Wirklichkeit. Stuttgart, Weimar: Metzler.

Atmanspacher, H., and Dalenoort, G. J. (1994). Inside versus Outside. Springer Verlag.

Bateson, G. (1972). "Form, substance, and difference," in Steps to an Ecology of Mind (448-466). New York: Ballantine.

Bell, J. (1994). "George Francis FitzGerald," Physics World **5**, 31-35.

Berliner, H., Goetsch, G., Campbell, M., and Ebeling, C. (1990). "Measuring the performance potential of chess programs," Artificial Intelligence, 43:7- 21.

Brandes, J. (1995). Die relativistischen Paradoxien und Thesen zu Raum und Zeit: Interpretationen der speziellen und allgemeinen Relativitätstheorie, 2. Aufl., Karlsbad: Verlag Relativistischer Interpretationen.

Bratko, I., and Michie, D. (1980). "A representation of pattern-knowledge in chess endgames," M.R.B. Clarke (ed), Advances in Computer Chess 2, 31-54. Edinburgh University Press.

Brooks, R. A. (1987). "Intelligence without representation," MIT Artificial Intelligence Report, 1987.

Buccheri, R. (2003). "The Intelligibility of Nature, the Endophysical Paradigm and the Relationship Between Physical an Psychological Time," The Nature of Time: Geometry, Physics and Perception, R. Buccheri, M. Saniga, W. M. Stuckey (eds), NATO Science Series II, **95**, pp 403-416.

Bohm, D. (1951). Quantum Theory. Prentice-Hall, New York.

Bohm, D. (1980). Wholeness and the Implicate Order, London: Routledge and Keagan Paul.

Bohm, D., and Hiley, B. (1993). The Undivided Universe: An Ontological Interpretation of Quantum Theory. London

Bohr, N. (1928). "Das Quantenpostulat und die neueren Entwicklungen in der Atomistik," Die Naturwissenschaften 16, 245-257.

Brentano, F. (1874). Psychology from an Empirical Standpoint. London: Routledge and Kegan Paul.

Chalmers, D.J. (1995), "Facing up to the problem of consciousness", Journal of Consciousness Studies, **2** (3), pp.200-19.

Chase, W., and Simon, H. (1972). "The mind's eye in chess," In W.G. Chase (ed), Visual Information Processing: Proceedings of the 8th Annual Carnegie Psychology Symposium. Academic Press, New York. Reprinted in Collins (ed.), Readings in Cognitive Science, Morgan Kaufmann 1988.

Collins, A. M., and Quillian, M. R. (1969). "Retrieval time from semantic memory," Journal of Verbal Learning and Verbal Behavior, 8:240-248.

Condon, J., and Thompson, K. (1982). "Belle chess hardware," In M.R.B. Clarke, editor, Advances in Computer Chess 3, pages 45-54. Pergamon Press.

Crutchfield, J., and Young, K. (1989). "Computation at the onset of Chaos," In W. Zurek (ed.), Complexity, entropy and the physics of information. Reading, MA: Addison-Wesley.

Crutchfield, J. (1992). "Knowledge and meaning… chaos and complexity," in Modeling Complex Phenomena, L. Lam and V. Naroditsky (eds.), Springer, Berlin.

Crick, F. and Koch, C. (1990), "Toward a neurobiological theory of consciousness," Seminars in the Neurosciences, **2**, pp.263-75.

deGroot, A. (1965). Thought and Choice in Chess. Mouton, The Hague.

deGroot, A., and Gobet, F. (1966). Perception and Memory in Chess. Van Gorcum, Assen, The Netherlands.

Donninger, C. (1996). "CHE: A graphical language for expressing chess knowledge," ICCA Journal, 19(4):234-241.

Ditto, W. and Pecora, L. (1993). "Mastering Chaos," Scientific American, 269, **2**, pp. 62-68.

Ebeling, C. (1987). All the Right Moves: A VLSI Architecture for Chess. The ACM Distinguished Dissertation Series. MIT Press.

Ehrlichson, H. (1973). "The Rod Contraction-Clock Retardation Ether Theory and the Special Theory of Relativity," Am. J. Phys. **41**, 1068-1077.

Einstein, A. (1905). "Zur Elektrodynamik bewegter Körper," Annalen der Physik **16**, 895-896.

Einstein, A. (1907). "On the Relativity Principle and the Conclusions Drawn from it," Jahrbuch der Radioaktivität und Elektronik **4**, 411-462.

Einstein, A. (1916). "Die Grundlagen der allgemeinen Relativitätstheorie", Annalen der Physik **49**, 769-822.

Einstein, A., Podolsky, B., and Rosen, N. (1935). "Can quantum-mechanical description of physical reality be considered complete?" Physical Review **47**, 777-780.

Emmeche, C., Køppe, S., Stjernfelt, F. (2000), "Levels, Emergence, and Three Versions of Downward Causation", Downward Causation. Minds, Bodies and Matter, P. B. Andersen, C. Emmeche, N. O. Finnemann and P. V. Christiansen (eds), Århus: Aarhus University Press, pp. 13-34.

Förster, H. (1985). Sicht und Einsicht. Versuche zu einer operativen Erkenntnistheorie. Braunschweig/Wiesbaden: Vieweg.

Ford, D.H. (1987), Humans as Self-constructing Living Systems. A Developmental Perspective on Behavior and Personality, Hillsdale (N.J.)-Hove-London: Lawrence Erlbaum Associates.

Franck, G. (2003). "How Time Passes," The Nature of Time: Geometry, Physics and Perception, R. Buccheri, M. Saniga, W. M. Stuckey (eds), NATO Science Series II, **95**, pp 91-104.

Fuchs, Christian (2003) "Dialectical Materialism and the Self-Organisation of Matter," Seeking Wisdom, Vol. 1 (2003), No. 1, pp. 25-55.

Foder, J., and Lepore, E. (1992). Holism: A Shopper's Guide. Cambridge, MA: Basil Blackwell.

Gardner, H. (1988). The Mind's New Science: A History of the Cognitive Revolution, Basic Books, New York.

George, M., and Schaeffer, J. (1990). "Chunking for experience," ICCA Journal, 13(3):123-132.

Gillogly, J. (1972). The technology chess program. Artificial Intelligence, 3:145-163.

Glaserfeld, E. (1990). "Die Unterscheidung des Beobachters: Versuch einer Auslegung," in Riegas, Vetter (eds) Zur Biologie der Kognition. Frankfurt/M. Suhrkamp, 95-123.

Gleick, J. (1988). Chaos – die Ordnung des Universums. München.

Gobet, F. (1993). "A computer model of chess memory," In Proceedings of the 15th Annual Meeting of the Cognitive Science Society, pages 463-468.

Gobet, F., and Jansen, P. (1994). "Towards a chess program based on a model of human memory," In H. J. van den Herik, I. S. Herschberg, and J. W. H. M. Uiterwijk, editors, Advances in Computer Chess 7, pages 35-60. University of Limburg.

Gobet, F., and Simon, H. (1996). "Templates in chess memory: A mechanism for recalling several boards," Cognitive Psychology, 31:1-40.

Grassberger, P. (1989). "Problems in quantifying self-generated complexity," Helvetica Physica Acta 62, 489-511.

Haken, H. (1981). Erfolgsgeheimnisse der Natur. Synergetik - Die Lehre vom Zusammenwirken. Stuttgart: Deutsche Verlagsanstalt.

Hawking, S. (1988). A Brief History of Time, London: Bantam.

Hayes, J. (1987). "Memory organization and world-class performance," In Proceedings of the 21st Carnegie-Mellon Symposium in Cognition.

Hejl, P. (1994). "Konstruktion der sozialen Konstruktion: Grundlagen einer konstruktivistischen Sozialtheorie," in S.J. Schmidt (ed) Der Diskurs des Radikalen Konstruktivismus. Frankfurt am Main, Suhrkamp.

Hoffmann, L. (1984). Grundlagen der Familientherapie. Hamburg, ISKO.

Holding, D. (1985). The Psychology of Chess Skill. Lawrence Erlbaum Associates.

Hsu, F.-H. (1987). "A two-million moves/s CMOS single-chip chess move generator," IEEE Journal of Solid-State Circuits, 22(5):841-846.

Hyatt, R., Gower, B.,and Nelson, H. (1985). "Cray Blitz," In Don Beal, editor, Advances in Computer Chess 4, pages 8-18. Pergamon Press, Oxford, UK.

Jammer, M. (1974). The Philosophy of Quantum Mechanics: The Interpretations of Quantum Mechanics in Historical Perspective. New York.

Junghanns, A., and Schaeffer, J. (1997). "Search versus knowledge in game-playing programs revisited," In Proceedings of the 15th International Joint Conference on Artificial Intelligence, Nagoya, Japan.

Kaindl, H. (1982). „Positional long-range planning in computer chess," In M. R. B. Clarke, editor, Advances in Computer Chess 3, pages 145-167. Pergamon Press.

Kerner, Y. (1994). „Case-based evaluation in computer chess." In M. Keane, J.P. Haton, and M. Manago, editors, Topics in Case-Based Reasoning (EWCBR-94), Lecture Notes in Artificial Intelligence, Berlin, Springer-Verlag.

Kerner, Y. (1995). „Learning strategies for explanation patterns: Basic game patterns with application to chess." In M. Veloso and A. Aamodt, editors, Proceedings of the 1st International Conference on Case-Based Reasoning (ICCBR-95), volume 1010 of Lecture Notes in Artificial Intelligence, pages 491-500, Berlin, Springer-Verlag.

Klimesch, W. (1994). The Structure of Long-Term Memory: A Connectivity Model of Semantic Processing. Lawrence Erlbaum Associates, Hillsdale, NJ.

Laplace, P. (1820). Essai Philosophique sur les Probabilités; forming the introduction to his Théorie Analytique des Probabilités, Paris: V Courcier; repr. F.W. Truscott and F.L. Emory (trans.), A Philosophical Essay on Probabilities, New York: Dover, 1951 .

Levy, D. (1988). editor. Computer Chess Compendium. Batsford Ltd., London.

Lorentz, H. (1909). The Theory of Electrons and its Applications to the Phenomena of Light and Radiant Heat. Columbia U. P. (1909).

Lorenz, K. (1973). Die Rückseite des Spiegels. Versuch einer Naturgeschichte menschlichen Erkennens. München-Zürich: Piper.

Luhmann, N. (1987). Soziale Systeme - Grundriß einer allgemeinen Theorie. Suhrkamp, 1987.

Mahler, G. (1997). "Nonlocality in quantum dynamics," in Time, Temporality, Now, Atmanspacher and Ruhnau (eds.), Berlin, Springer.

Mandelblit, N., and Zachar, O. (1988). "The Notion of Dynamic Unit: Conceptual Developments in Cognitive Science," Cognitive Science **22** (2).

Mandelbrot, B. (1987). Die fraktale Geometrie der Natur. Birkhäuser, Basel.

Maturana, H., and Varela, F. (1987). The Tree of Knowledge, Boston: Shambhala.

May, R. (1989). Heidegger's Hidden Sources (tr. by G. Parkes, London and New York: Routledge 1996).

McTaggart, J. (1908). "The unreality of time," in : Mind, New Series 68, pp. 457-474.

Michie, D., and Bratko, I. (1991). "Comments to 'chunking for experience." ICCA Journal, 18(1):18, March 1991.

Minkowski, H. (1915). "Raum und Zeit," in „Das Relativitätsprinzip", Teubner, Leipzig, English: "Space and Time," in The Principle of Relativity," Dover, Ney York (1952).

Misner, C., Thorne, K., and Wheeler, J. (1973). Gravitation, San Franzisco: Freeman, 170-172.

Muggleton, S. (1988). "Inductive acquisition of chess strategies." In J. E. Hayes, D. Michie, and J. Richards, editors, Machine Intelligence 11, chapter 17, pages 375-387. Clarendon Press.

Newell, A., and Simon, H. (1976). "Computer Science as empirical inquiry: Symbols and search," Communications of the ACM, 19, 3, 113-126.

Newell, A., Shaw, C., and Simon, H. (1958). Chess playing programs and the problem of complexity. IBM Journal of Research and Development, 2:320-335, October 1958. Reprinted in (Levy, 1988).

Nichols, M., and Schwartz, R. (1998). Family Therapy: Concepts and Methods. Fourth Edition. Allyn & Bacon.

Nunn, J. (1992). Secrets of Rook Endings. Batsford, 1992.

Nunn, J. (1994a). "Extracting information from endgame databases." In H. J. van den Herik, I. S. Herschberg, and J. W. H. M. Uiterwijk, editors, Advances in Computer Chess 7, pages 19-34. University of Limburg.

Nunn, J. (1994b). Secrets of Pawnless Endings. Batsford.

Nunn, J. (1995). Secrets of Minor-Piece Endings. Batsford.

Opdahl, A., and Tessem, B. (1994). "Long-term planning in computer chess." In H. J. van den Herik, I. S. Herschberg, and J. W. H. M. Uiterwijk, editors, Advances in Computer Chess 7. University of Limburg.

Packard, N., Crutchfield, J., et al. (1980). Phys. Rev. Letters **45**, 712.

Pauli, W. (1958). Theory of Relativity, Pergamon Press, 130-134.

Piaget, J. (1975). Der Aufbau der Wirklichkeit beim Kinde. Gesammelte Werke, Band 2. Stuttgart: Klett.

Popper, K. (1982). Quantum Theory and The Schism in Physics. New Jersey, US: Rowman and Littlefield, **25**.

Pribram, K. (1976). Consciousness and the Brain. Plenum, New York.

Price, H. (1996). Time's Arrow & Archimedes' Point, New York: Oxford University Press.

Prigogine, I., and Stengers, I. (1984). Order Out of Chaos - Man´s New Dialogue with Nature. Bantam Books, 1984.

Primas, H. (1993). "The Cartesian cut, the Heisenberg cut, and disentangled observers," in Symposium on the Foundations of Modern Physics 1992: Wolfgang Pauli as a Philosopher, ed. by Laurikainen and C. Montonen, World Scientific, Singapore.

Recami, E. (1987). "Tachyon Kinematics and Causality: A Systematic Thorough Analysis of the Tachyon Causal Paradoxes," Found. Phys. **17**(3), 241-296.

Roycroft, A. (1988). "Expert against oracle." In J. E. Hayes, D. Michie, and J. Richards, editors, Machine Intelligence 11, pages 347-373. Oxford University Press, Oxford, UK.

Schmidt, S. (1987). ed. Der Diskurs des Radikalen Konstruktivismus 2. Suhrkamp.

Schmidt, S. (1992). ed. Kognition und Gesellschaft - Der Diskurs des Radikalen Konstruktivismus 2. Suhrkamp.

Seager, W. (1995), "Consciousness, information and panpsychism", Journal of Consciousness Studies, **2** (3), pp.272-80.

Searle, J. (1980). "Minds, Brains and Programs," Behavioral and Brain Sciences **3**, 417-424.

Searle, J. (1992). The Rediscovery of the Mind. MIT press, pp. 111-112;

Shannon, C. (1948). "A mathematical theory of communication," Bell System Technical Journal, vol. 27, pp. 379-423 and 623-656, July and October, 1948.

Shannon, C. (1950). "Programming a computer for playing chess." Philosophical Magazine, 41(7):256-275, 1950. Reprinted in (Levy, 1988).

Simon, H., and Barenfeld, M. (1969). „Information-processing analysis of perceptual processes in problem solving." Psychological Review, 76(5):473-483.

Simon, H., and Chase, W. (1973). "Skill in chess." American Scientist, 61(4):394-403.

Simon, H., and Gilmartin, K. (1973). "A simulation of memory for chess positions." Cognitive Psychology, 5:29-46.

Slate, D., and Atkin, L. (1983). "Chess 4.5 -- the northwestern university chess program." In Chess Skill in Man and Machine, chapter 4, pages 82-118. Springer-Verlag, 2nd edition.

Smolensky, P. (1988). "On the proper treatment of connectionism." Behavior and Brain Sciences II, 1-74.

Stanley, L., and Wise, S. (1983). Breaking Out: Feminist Consciousness and Feminist Research. London: Routledge and Kegan Paul.

Svozil, K. (1994). "Extrinsic-Intrinsic Concept and Complementarity," in Inside versus Outside. Atmanspacher&Dalenoort (eds), Springer, 273-288.

Svozil, K. (2000). "Relativizing Relativity," Found. Phys. **30**(7), 1001-1016.

Takens, F. (1981). "Detecting strange attractors in turbulence", Dynamical Systems and Turbulence, Warwick 1980, Lecture Notes in Math. 898, 366-381.

Turing, A. (1950). "Computing Machinery and Intelligence" Mind 59, 236, 433-60.

Turing, A. (1953). "Chess." In B.V. Bowden, editor, Faster Than Thought, pages 286-295. Bitman, London, 1953. Reprinted in (Levy, 1988).

Wilkins, D. (1980). "Using patterns and plans in chess." Artificial Intelligence, 14(3):165-203.

Wilkins, D. (1982). "Using knowledge to control tree search searching." Artificial Intelligence, 18(1):1-51.

Winkler, F.-G. (1991). Das Vernetzungsmodell von Klimesch - eine Simulation. Master's thesis, Institute for Medical Cybernetics and Artificial Intelligence, University of Vienna, Vienna, Austria.

Winkler, F.-G. (1995). "Meaningful Representation? - A dynamical systems approach and some implications for cognitive science," Proceedings of the workshop on cognitive science, AISB 1995, Sheffield.

Winkler, F.-G. (1996). "Contradiction - From Causal Flow to Infinite Ontology." in Cybernetics and Systems Research '96, Trappl (ed.), Proceedings of the 14th European Meeting on Cybernetics and Systems Research, Vienna, April 1996, **2**, 471-476.

Winkler, F.-G., and Fürnkranz, J. (1998). "On Effort in AI Research: A Description Along Two Dimensions," ICCA Journal, March 1998.

Winkler, F.-G. (1998). "From Relativity to Duality - A Holistic Perspective," in Cybernetics and Systems '98, R. Trappl (ed), Proceedings of the 14th European Meeting on Cybernetics and Systems Research, Vienna, April 1998, **2**, 872-877.

Winkler, F.-G. (1999). "Space-Time Unity and the Representation Problem," Computing Anticipatory Systems: Daniel Dubois (ed.), American Institute of Physics, Woodburg, New York, Conference Proceedings **465**, 131-141.

Winkler, F.-G. (2002a). "An Outside View of Space and Time". International Journal of Computing Anticipatory Systems, D. Dubois (ed.), **11**, 229-241.

Winkler, F.-G. (2002b). "The Normalization Problem of Special Relativity," Physics Essays, **15** (2).

Winkler, F.-G, (2003) "Spacetime Holism and the Passage of Time", The Nature of Time: Geometry, Physics and Perception, R. Buccheri, M. Saniga, W. M. Stuckey (eds), NATO Science Series II, **95**, 393-402.

Varela, F., Thompson, E., and Rosch, E. (1991). The Embodied Mind. MIT press.

Zobrist, A., and Carlson, F. (1973). "An advice-taking chess computer." Scientific American, 93-105, June 1973.

VDM Verlagsservicegesellschaft mbH

Die VDM Verlagsservicegesellschaft sucht für wissenschaftliche Verlage abgeschlossene und herausragende

Dissertationen, Habilitationen, Diplomarbeiten, Master Theses, Magisterarbeiten usw.

für die kostenlose Publikation als Fachbuch.

Sie verfügen über eine Arbeit, die hohen inhaltlichen und formalen Ansprüchen genügt, und haben Interesse an einer honorarvergüteten Publikation?

Dann senden Sie bitte erste Informationen über sich und Ihre Arbeit per Email an *info@vdm-vsg.de*.

Sie erhalten kurzfristig unser Feedback!

VDM Verlagsservicegesellschaft mbH
Dudweiler Landstr. 99
D - 66123 Saarbrücken
Telefon +49 681 3720 174
Fax +49 681 3720 1749
www.vdm-vsg.de

Die VDM Verlagsservicegesellschaft mbH vertritt

Printed by Books on Demand GmbH, Norderstedt / Germany